EVOLVE

STUDENT'S BOOK

with Practice Extra

Ben Goldstein and Ceri Jones

4B

CAMBRIDGE
UNIVERSITY PRESS

CAMBRIDGE
UNIVERSITY PRESS

University Printing House, Cambridge CB2 8BS, United Kingdom

One Liberty Plaza, 20th Floor, New York, NY 10006, USA

477 Williamstown Road, Port Melbourne, VIC 3207, Australia

314–321, 3rd Floor, Plot 3, Splendor Forum, Jasola District Centre, New Delhi – 110025, India

79 Anson Road, #06–04/06, Singapore 079906

Cambridge University Press is part of the University of Cambridge.

It furthers the University's mission by disseminating knowledge in the pursuit of education, learning, and research at the highest international levels of excellence.

www.cambridge.org
Information on this title: www.cambridge.org/9781108409254

First published 2019

20 19 18 17 16 15 14 13 12 11 10 9 8 7 6 5 4 3 2

Printed in Great Britain by CPI (UK) Ltd. Croydon CRO 4YY

A catalogue record for this publication is available from the British Library

ISBN 978-1-108-40531-7 Student's Book
ISBN 978-1-108-40509-6 Student's Book A
ISBN 978-1-108-40923-0 Student's Book B
ISBN 978-1-108-40532-4 Student's Book with Practice Extra
ISBN 978-1-108-40510-2 Student's Book with Practice Extra A
ISBN 978-1-108-40925-4 Student's Book with Practice Extra B
ISBN 978-1-108-40901-8 Workbook with Audio
ISBN 978-1-108-40874-5 Workbook with Audio A
ISBN 978-1-108-41194-3 Workbook with Audio B
ISBN 978-1-108-40518-8 Teacher's Edition with Test Generator
ISBN 978-1-108-41071-7 Presentation Plus
ISBN 978-1-108-41204-9 Class Audio CDs
ISBN 978-1-108-40795-3 Video Resource Book with DVD
ISBN 978-1-108-41449-4 Full Contact with DVD
ISBN 978-1-108-41155-4 Full Contact A with DVD
ISBN 978-1-108-41417-3 Full Contact B with DVD

Additional resources for this publication at www.cambridge.org/evolve

Cambridge University Press has no responsibility for the persistence or accuracy of URLs for external or third-party internet websites referred to in this publication, and does not guarantee that any content on such websites is, or will remain, accurate or appropriate. Information regarding prices, travel timetables, and other factual information given in this work is correct at the time of first printing but Cambridge University Press does not guarantee the accuracy of such information thereafter.

ACKNOWLEDGMENTS

To our student contributors, who have given us their ideas and their time, and who appear throughout this book:

Andres Ramírez Fabian, Mexico; Alessandra Avelar, Brazil; Nicolle Juliana Torres Sierra, Colombia; Ouattara Maryne Soukeina, USA; Seung Geyong Yang, South Korea; Tayra Laritza Lacayo Sanchez, Honduras.

Author

The authors and publishers acknowledge the following sources of copyright material and are grateful for the permissions granted. While every effort has been made, it has not always been possible to identify the sources of all the material used, or to trace all copyright holders. If any omissions are brought to our notice, we will be happy to include the appropriate acknowledgements on reprinting and in the next update to the digital edition, as applicable.

Photographs

B = Below, BC = Below Centre, BG = Background, BL = Below Left, BR = Below Right, CL = Centre Left, CR = Centre Right, TC = Top Centre, TL = Top Left, TR = Top Right.

The following photographs are sourced from Getty Images.

p. xvi (TR): asiseeit/E+; p. xvi (BL): vlada_maestro/iStock/Getty Images Plus; pp. 74, 84, 94, 106, 116, 126: Tom Merton/Caiaimage; p. 104 (TL): Westend61; p. 65: Antonio_Diaz/iStock/Getty Images Plus; p. 66: Matt Cardy/Getty Images News; p. 69: Jasmin Awad/EyeEm; p. 70 (photo 1): Fotosearch; p. 70 (photo 2): Zac Macaulay/Cultura/Getty Images Plus; p. 72 (emoji): Pingebat/iStock/Getty Images Plus; p. 72 (TR): Christophe Morin/IP3/Getty Images News; p. 74 (smartphone): Tim Robberts/The Image Bank; p. 74 (concert): Isabella Torreallba/EyeEm; p. 75: PATRICK KOVARIK/AFP; p. 77 (BL): Stephane Godin/Biosphoto; p. 77 (BR): hardyuno/iStock/Getty Images Plus; p. 77: Roderick Chen/All Canada Photos; p. 80 (photo 1): Jessica Peterson; p. 80 (photo 2): Eduard Titov/Moment; p. 81: David Arky; p. 82 (TL): Klaus Vedfelt/The Image Bank; p. 82 (TR): Cultura Exclusive/Moof; p. 83: John Fedele/Blend Images; p. 84: Jonathan Kitchen/DigitalVision; p. 85 (stop sign): Dallas Stribley/Lonely Planet Images; p. 85 (BR): Bernard Van Berg/EyeEm; p. 88 (TL): Dave Walsh/VW Pics/UIG; p. 88 (TC): Philippe Marion/Moment; p. 88 (TR): Grant Faint/The Image Bank; p. 88 (carriages): Charles Phelps Cushing/ClassicStock/Archive Photos; p. 90: Peter Muller/Cultura; p. 91: Richard Baker/In Pictures; p. 93: Andersen Ross/Blend Images; p. 94 (TL): baranozdemir/iStock/Getty Images Plus; p. 94 (TC): Creatas/Getty Images Plus; p. 96: Dev Carr/Cultura; p. 97: National Geographic; p. 98 (army): holgs/E+; p. 98 (microwave): Bettmann; p. 99: Hinterhaus Productions/DigitalVision; p. 100 (TL): Kevin Winter/Getty Images Entertainment; p. 100 (TR): Allsport/Hulton Archive; p. 101 (BL): Debra Bardowicks/Oxford Scientific; p. 101 (BC): Image Source; p. 101 (BR): Peter Cade/The Image Bank; p. 102 (TC): Yagi-Studio/E+; p. 102 (TR): Kyle Monk/Blend Images; p. 103: WendellandCarolyn/iStock/Getty Images Plus; p. 104 (TR): Henrik Weis/DigitalVision; p. 105: Michael Schwalbe/EyeEm; p. 106 (fire): Moritz Witter/EyeEm; p. 106 (hieroglyphics): Raffi Maghdessian; p. 106 (syringe): AtomicCupcake/DigitalVision Vectors; p. 106 (corn): Diane Labombarbe/DigitalVision Vectors; p. 106 (laptop): hudiemm/DigitalVision Vectors; p. 106 (atom): bortonia/DigitalVision Vectors; p. 107: Alija/iStock/Getty Images Plus; p. 108 (BG): johns0114/johns0114; p. 108 (CR): Elliott Kaufman/Corbis; p. 108 (TL): LWA/Dann Tardif/Blend Images; p. 108 (Lee): YinYang/E+; p. 108 (Allie): moodboard/Getty Images Plus; p. 110 (carrot): rimglow/iStock/Getty Images Plus; p. 110 (cheese): vikif/iStock/Getty Images Plus; p. 110 (honey): Miro Vrlik/EyeEm; p. 111: VladGans/E+; p. 112 (spray): Madmaxer/iStock/Getty Images Plus; p. 112 (candle): Blanchi Costela/Moment; p. 112 (patch): Fahroni/iStock/Getty Images Plus; p. 113 (photo 1): ljpat/iStock/Getty Images Plus; p. 113 (photo 2): kevinjeon00/E+; p. 113 (photo 3): DarioEgidi/iStock/Getty Images Plus; p. 114: metamorworks/iStock/Getty Images Plus; p. 115: VCG/Getty Images News; p. 116: Anton Petrus/Moment; p. 117: Allan Baxter/Photographer's Choice; p. 118 (photo a): Mark Edward Atkinson/Tracey Lee/Blend Images; p. 118 (photo b): Sladic/iStock/Getty Images Plus; p. 118 (photo c), p. 74 (girl): KidStock/Blend Images; p. 119: Rhydian Lewis/Photographer's Choice; p. 120: Barbara Ferra Fotografia/Moment; p. 121 (rollerskates): Peathegee Inc/Blend Images; p. 121 (console): Andy Crawford/Dorling Kindersley; p. 121 (tireswing): sarahwolfephotography/Moment Open; p. 122: SeventyFour/iStock/Getty Images Plus; p. 124 (photo a): PEDRO PARDO/AFP; p. 124 (photo b): altrendo images; p. 124 (photo c): Paul Park/Moment; p. 124 (photo d): Jupiterimages/Stockbyte; p. 126: Eddy LEMAISTRE/Corbis Sport.

Below photographs are sourced from other libraries:

p. 76: © Tasmania 360/Loic Le Guilly; p. 92: © Tim Griffith (photographer) and LMS (architects). Reproduced with permission; p. 94 (TR): keith morris/Alamy Stock Photo; p. 128: image anorak/Alamy Stock Photo.

Front cover photography by Alija/E+/Getty Images.

Illustrations by Ana Djordjevic (Astound US) pp. 86; Mark Duffin (ODI) p. 68; 290 Sean (KJA Artists) p. 87.

Audio production by CityVox, New York.

EVOLVE

SPEAKING MATTERS

EVOLVE is a six-level American English course for adults and young adults, taking students from beginner to advanced levels (CEFR A1 to C1).

Drawing on insights from language teaching experts and real students, EVOLVE is a general English course that gets students speaking with confidence.

This student-centered course covers all skills and focuses on the most effective and efficient ways to make progress in English.

Confidence in teaching.
Joy in learning.

Better Learning WITH EVOLVE

Better Learning is our simple approach where insights we've gained from research have helped shape content that drives results. Language evolves, and so does the way we learn. This course takes a flexible, student-centered approach to English language teaching.

EVOLVE
STUDENT'S BOOK
Ben Goldstein and Ceri Jones
4

BRIDGE

Experience
Better
Learning

Meet our student contributors ▶

Videos and ideas from real students feature throughout the Student's Book.

Our student contributors describe themselves in three words.

SEUNG GEYOUNG YANG

Happy, creative
Myongji University,
South Korea

ANDRES RAMÍREZ FABIAN

Friendly, happy, funny
Instituto Tecnológico
de Morelia, México

OUATTARA MARYNE SOUKEINA

Friendly, perfectionist, creative
Educational Language Services,
USA

ALESSANDRA AVELAR

Creative, positive, funny
Faculdade ICESP, Águas
Claras, Brazil

TAYRA LARITZA LACAYO SANCHEZ

Tenacious, oustanding, curious
La universidad global
de Honduras

NICOLLE JULIANA TORRES SIERRA

Passionate, Friendly, committed
Cenrtro Colombo Americano,
Colombia

Student-generated content

EVOLVE is the first course of its kind to feature real student-generated content. We spoke to over 2,000 students from all over the world about the topics they would like to discuss in English and in what situations they would like to be able to speak more confidently.

The ideas are included throughout the Student's Book and the students appear in short videos responding to discussion questions.

INSIGHT

Research shows that achievable speaking role models can be a powerful motivator.

CONTENT

Bite-sized videos feature students talking about topics in the Student's Book.

RESULT

Students are motivated to speak and share their ideas.

"It's important to provide learners with interesting or stimulating topics."

Teacher, Mexico (Global Teacher Survey, 2017)

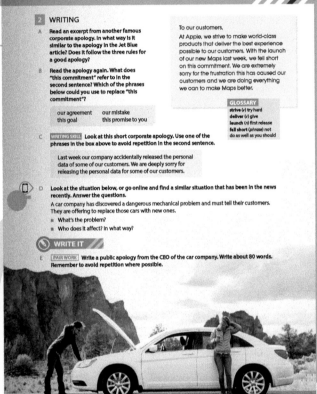

Find it

FIND IT

INSIGHT

Research with hundreds of teachers and students across the globe revealed a desire to expand the classroom and bring the real world in.

CONTENT

Find it are smartphone activities that allow students to bring live content into the class and personalize the learning experience with research and group activities.

RESULT

Students engage in the lesson because it is meaningful to them.

Designed for success

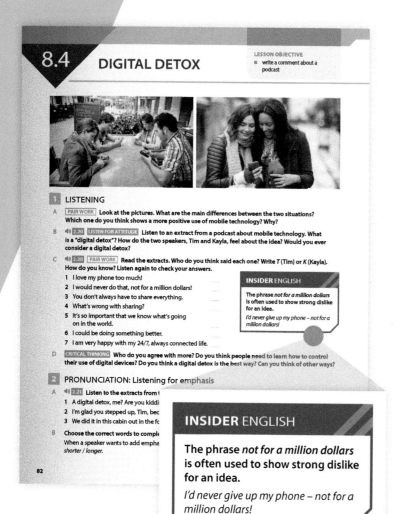

INSIDER ENGLISH

The phrase *not for a million dollars* is often used to show strong dislike for an idea.

I'd never give up my phone – not for a million dollars!

Pronunciation

INSIGHT

Research shows that only certain aspects of pronunciation actually affect comprehensibility and inhibit communication.

CONTENT

EVOLVE focuses on the aspects of pronunciation that most affect communication.

RESULT

Students understand more when listening and can be clearly understood when they speak.

Insider English

INSIGHT

Even in a short exchange, idiomatic language can inhibit understanding.

CONTENT

Insider English focuses on the informal language and colloquial expressions frequently found in everyday situations.

RESULT

Students are confident in the real world.

8.1 THE PERFECT JOB?

LESSON OBJECTIVE
■ talk about different working lifestyles

1 LANGUAGE IN CONTEXT

A Look at the picture and its caption in the post below. What job is the ad for? Read the full post. Is the writer interested in applying for the job? Why or why not?

> **If you saw this job ad on your timeline, would you click to find out more? I did, along with 300,000 other people!**
>
> The island of Maatsuyker in Tasmania is looking for two temporary caretakers to live on the island for six months each. No television or internet access. The work is not very stressful, as the lighthouse runs automatically. The caretaker's job is basically to report on data from the weather station, so it's not a tough job. It rains a lot, but the views and the wildlife are amazing. Everybody who visits falls in love with the island.
>
>
> Island seeks lighthouse caretaker for six months.
> *Click here* to apply!
>
> What was your first reaction? Would you enjoy being cut off from the rest of the world for six months? Does that sound like your dream job? I'm not so sure I could do it! Maybe if I was single and didn't have kids I might do it. But with a family, I need a permanent job – preferably one that's high-paying! What about you? If you were free to do it, would you apply for this job?

B **PAIR WORK** Do you think you could do the job described in the ad? Why or why not? You can use your phones to find out more about the island before you answer.

2 VOCABULARY: Describing jobs

A 🔊 2.11 **PAIR WORK** Listen and say the words in the box. Which ones are in the post? Do they have a positive or negative meaning? What about the other words? Look them up in a dictionary or on your phone if needed.

challenging	desk job	dream job	freelance	full-time
government job	high-paying	main job	part-time	permanent
second job	stressful	temporary	tiring	tough

B Which words in the box are useful to give a factual description of a job? Underline them. Which words express an opinion? Circle them.

C ▶ Now go to page 148. Do the vocabulary exercises for 8.1.

D **PAIR WORK** Describe the jobs in the box using the descriptions in exercise A.

babysitter	doctor	firefighter
lifeguard	fashion designer	sales assistant

> Well, being a babysitter is probably a part-time job, and it isn't very high-paying, but it is very challenging.

3 GRAMMAR: Present unreal conditionals

A Read the sentences in the grammar box. Then complete the rules.

> **Present unreal conditionals**
>
> If you **saw** this ad on your timeline, **would** you **click** to find out more?
>
> If you **were** free to do it, **would** you **apply** for this job?
>
> If I **was** single and **didn't have** kids and **wanted** to write a book or something, I **might do** it.

> **REGISTER CHECK**
>
> In formal language, use *were* for all subjects, including 1st and 3rd person.
> *If I were selected, I would devote myself to it.*
> In informal language, you can use *was* for 1st and 3rd person subjects.
> *If I / she was feeling better, I / she would go.*

1 The sentences refer to **a real / an imagined** situation.
2 Look at the **bold** verbs. The verb form that follows *if* is **simple present / simple past.** It **refers / doesn't refer** to a past situation.

B ▶ Now go to page 136. Look at the grammar chart and do the grammar exercise for 8.1.

C **PAIR WORK** Complete the questions with the correct form of the **verb in parentheses ( ).** Ask and answer the questions with your partner.

1 If you _____ (can do) any job in the world, what job _____ you _____ (choose)? Why?
2 _____ you _____ (consider) doing a job you loved if you _____ (not be) paid well? Why or why not?
3 What _____ you _____ (do) with your free time if you _____ (not have to) work?

4 SPEAKING

A Read about two more jobs. How are they similar to the lighthouse caretaker job?

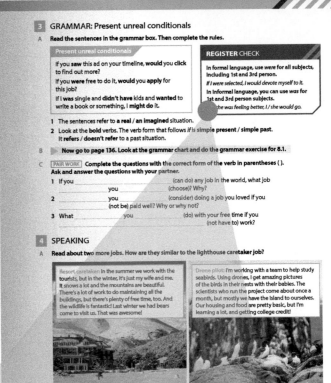

Resort caretaker: In the summer we work with the tourists, but in the winter, it's just my wife and me. It snows a lot and the mountains are beautiful. There's a lot of work to do maintaining all the buildings, but there's plenty of free time, too. And the wildlife is fantastic! Last winter we had bears come to visit us. That was awesome!

Drone pilot: I'm working with a team to help study seabirds. Using drones, I get amazing pictures of the birds in their nests with their babies. The scientists who run the project come about once a month, but mostly we have the island to ourselves. Our housing and food are pretty basic, but I'm learning a lot, and getting college credit!

B **PAIR WORK** If you had to choose one of the three jobs in this lesson, which one would you choose? Why? What do you think daily life would be like?

REGISTER CHECK

In formal language, use *were* for all subjects, including 1st and 3rd person.

If I were selected, I would devote myself to it.

In informal language, you can use *was* for 1st and 3rd person subjects.

If I / she was feeling better, I / she would go.

Register check

INSIGHT

Teachers report that their students often struggle to master the differences between written and spoken English.

CONTENT

Register check draws on research into the Cambridge English Corpus and highlights potential problem areas for learners.

RESULT

Students transition confidently between written and spoken English and recognize different levels of formality as well as when to use them appropriately.

"The presentation is very clear and there are plenty of opportunities for student practice and production."

Jason Williams, Teacher, Notre Dame Seishin University, Japan

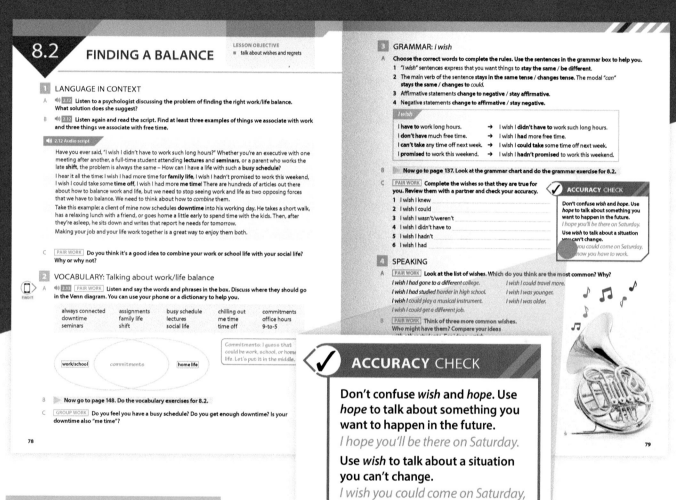

Accuracy check

INSIGHT

Some common errors can become fossilized if not addressed early on in the learning process.

CONTENT

Accuracy check highlights common learner errors (based on unique research into the Cambridge Learner Corpus) and can be used for self-editing.

RESULT

Students avoid common errors in their written and spoken English.

You spoke. We listened.

Students told us that speaking is the most important skill for them to master, while teachers told us that finding speaking activities which engage their students and work in the classroom can be challenging.

That's why EVOLVE has a whole lesson dedicated to speaking: Lesson 5, *Time to speak*.

Time to speak

INSIGHT

Speaking ability is how students most commonly measure their own progress, but is also the area where they feel most insecure. To be able to fully exploit speaking opportunities in the classroom, students need a safe speaking environment where they can feel confident, supported, and able to experiment with language.

CONTENT

Time to Speak is a unique lesson dedicated to developing speaking skills and is based around immersive tasks which involve information sharing and decision making.

RESULT

Time to speak lessons create a buzz in the classroom where speaking can really thrive, evolve, and take off, resulting in more confident speakers of English.

8.5

TIME TO SPEAK
Planning a digital detox

LESSON OBJECTIVE
- plan and discuss a digital detox weekend for your class

A **DISCUSS** As a class, discuss this question: If you had to live without your phone for a week, how would that affect your day-to-day life? Think of all the things you usually do with your phone. What would you miss the most?

B You and a partner are going to arrange a digital detox weekend for your class. Think of the answers your classmates gave. Who do you think would suffer the most from the detox? Why?

C A TV company is going to sponsor your weekend and make a documentary about the experience. Think about these things:
- Where could you hold the detox? Think of places in or near your city.
- What facilities would you need? Think of alternatives to digital devices, for example, a gym or a library.
- What activities would you like to offer? How could you help people when they're missing their phones? Think of a variety of different activities for both daytime and evening hours.

> There are some big houses by the beach. We'd need lots of bedrooms but just one kitchen. A gym would be great, and if we had a library, people could still read, just not on their tablets. Our experience is going to be filmed, so we should have some conflicts too, for drama, like some sports activities.

D **DECIDE** Create a plan for the weekend. Include this information:
- what time the program starts on Friday and ends on Sunday
- morning, afternoon, and evening activity choices for the full three days

E **PRESENT** Present your program to the class. Answer any questions from the audience.

F **AGREE** Which pair of students has planned the best program? Why do you think so?

>> *To check your progress, go to page 155.* >>

USEFUL PHRASES

DISCUSS
If I had to ..., I think I'd ...
I'd really miss ...
If we held the detox [place], then people might ...

DECIDE
I think we should / could ...
Why don't we ... ?
What about ... ?

PRESENT
We decided / thought that ...
We chose to ...
We want to / We'd like to ...

84

Experience Better Learning with EVOLVE: a course that helps both teachers and students on every step of the language learning journey.

Speaking matters. Find out more about creating safe speaking environments in the classroom.

EVOLVE unit structure

Unit opening page

Each unit opening page activates prior knowledge and vocabulary and immediately gets students speaking.

Lessons 1 and 2

These lessons present and practice the unit vocabulary and grammar in context, helping students discover language rules for themselves. Students then have the opportunity to use this language in well-scaffolded, personalized speaking tasks.

Lesson 3

This lesson is built around a functional language dialogue that models and contextualizes useful fixed expressions for managing a particular situation. This is a real world strategy to help students handle unexpected conversational turns.

Lesson 4

This is a combined skills lesson based around an engaging reading or listening text. Each lesson asks students to think critically and ends with a practical writing task.

Lesson 5

Time to speak is an entire lesson dedicated to developing speaking skills. Students work on collaborative, immersive tasks which involve information sharing and decision making.

CONTENTS

CLASSROOM LANGUAGE

PAIR WORK AND GROUP WORK

🔊 **1.02** **Choosing roles**

How should we start?

Why don't you be ... and I'll be ...

Who wants to present for our group?

Understanding the task

So what are we supposed to do?

I'm not really sure.

Should we ask the teacher?

Asking for more time

Sorry, we're not done yet. We need a few more minutes.

Completing a task

OK. So are we done with this part?

I think so. What's next?

TALKING TO THE TEACHER

Discussing assignments

When is ... due?

Can I email ... to you?

Discussing a missed class

I was out on ... Can you tell me what I missed?

Asking for explanations

Can you tell us what we're supposed to do again?

Can you explain that again? I didn't understand.

Preparing for a text/exam

Will this be on the test?

Will we review this before the test?

UNIT OBJECTIVES

- discuss the importance of messaging apps
- discuss written vs. spoken communication
- recount conversations, news, and stories
- write an email in a formal and informal register
- create and conduct a communication survey

CAN WE TALK?

7

START SPEAKING

A   Look at the picture. What is the man doing? How do you think the other people feel?

B   Is this a realistic situation? Why or why not? What does it say about the use of phones in our society?

C   What other situations can you think of where you shouldn't use your phone? For ideas, watch Seung Geyong's video.

REAL STUDENT

Do you agree with Seung Geyong?

A COMMON LANGUAGE

1 LANGUAGE IN CONTEXT

A **PAIR WORK** Look at the picture and the title of the article. What are the people doing? Where are they? Read and check your answers.

📱 Smartphone lifeline

We use smartphone apps to **keep in touch with** family, **catch up with** friends, **congratulate** people on special events, **respond to** invitations, and even **gossip** about our favorite celebrities.

But for migrants who leave their families behind in search of a better life, messaging apps provide the best (sometimes the only) way to **inform their families of** their progress. Many migrants have limited resources, but their relatives **persuade** them to buy a device. Refugee camps now provide charging stations. Greenpeace recently **reported** that use of their stations had increased greatly.

Some recent immigrants to the U.S. **commented** that WhatsApp had eased their sense of isolation. One new arrival **explained** that the app allowed him to **contact** his family: "I tell them about things I wouldn't have **mentioned** in a once-a-week phone call, and they can **reply to** me at once. You feel they are really close."

For most of us, smartphones apps make daily life easier and more fun, and we even **criticize** people for using them too much. For migrants, however, messaging apps are an absolute lifeline.

GLOSSARY
lifeline (*n*) something that you depend on

B **Choose the correct phrase to complete the statements.**
1 For migrants, a messaging app is often *a fun way / the only way* to communicate with family.
2 Charities now provide *charging stations / messaging apps* to help refugees stay in touch with family.

2 VOCABULARY: Describing communication

A 🔊 2.02 **Categorize the words in the box according to similar meaning. Listen and check.**

catch up with	comment	congratulate	contact
explain	gossip	inform of	reply to

A respond to, _____

B mention, report, _____ , _____ ,

_____

C keep in touch with, _____ , _____

D criticize, persuade, _____ , _____

B ▶ **Now go to page 147. Do the vocabulary exercises for 7.1.**

C **PAIR WORK** **Answer the questions.**
- How do you keep in touch with people who live far away?
- When was the last time that you congratulated a friend on something? What was it?
- When did you persuade somebody to do something? What was it?

3 GRAMMAR: Reported statements

A **Choose the best options to complete the rules. Use the sentences in the grammar box to help you.**

1 To report a present tense statement, use the **present** / **past**.

2 To report a past tense statement, use the **past** / **past perfect**.

3 To report a present perfect statement, use the **past** / **past perfect**.

4 To report instructions and suggestions, use the **present** / **past** + pronoun + (*not*) *to* + verb.

Reported statements

One new arrival explained that the app **allowed** him to contact his family.

Some immigrants commented that WhatsApp **had eased** their sense of isolation.

Greenpeace recently reported that use of their stations **had increased** greatly.

Their families **persuaded** them to buy a smartphone.

B ▶ **Now go to page 135. Look at the grammar chart and do the grammar exercise for 7.1.**

Now go to page 135. Look at the grammar chart and do the grammar exercise for 7.1.

C **PAIR WORK** **Take turns making statements that are true for you. Report your partner's statements.**

1 live with family

"I live with my family." Manny explained that he lived with his family.

2 know how to drive   4 see ocean

3 visit Spain   5 try app / not like it

D **PAIR WORK** **Think of things that you have heard about this week. How did you hear about them? Use reporting verbs to explain the news to your partner.**

> My brother mentioned that he had won a prize at school. We congratulated him.

> The media reported that unemployment is lower this quarter.

> **!** We usually change the tense of the verb when making reported statements, but when talking about facts, habits, or ongoing actions it is OK to keep the original tense.
>
> *"I'm going to buy a new phone."* She said she **is going to** buy a new phone.

---

4 SPEAKING

A **PAIR WORK** **How do you use messaging apps like WhatsApp? Check (✓) the statements that describe you. Then compare answers with a partner.**

☐ I use messaging apps for practical purposes only.

☐ I use them for all kinds of communication.

☐ I use them for work.

☐ If I really miss somebody, I prefer to call them.

☐ I don't use them. Having contact with people far away makes me miss them more.

☐ I only use written text. I don't like to leave voice messages.

☐ I use messaging apps to call people. Texting is too slow.

B **GROUP WORK** **Join another pair of students. Report your answers to the other pair. What similarities and differences did you find?**

> Bernard said that he used WhatsApp for everything, for work and pleasure.

> Celia stated that she only uses it for meeting friends.

7.2 TO TEXT OR NOT TO TEXT

LESSON OBJECTIVE
- discuss written vs. spoken communication

1 LANGUAGE IN CONTEXT

A 🔊 **2.03** **Read and listen to the first part of an interview about a research study on communication. What questions were people asked?**

🔊 **2.03 Audio script**

Host	On today's podcast, we look at some research on digital technology and how it is affecting how we communicate. We have here Professor Dorothy Zárraga from Brown University. Dr. Zárraga, tell us about your research.
Dr Zárraga	Well, we interviewed people from different age groups to see if different generations communicate differently.
Host	And what types of questions did you ask?
Dr Zárraga	We asked some questions about how they preferred to communicate. For example, we asked if they preferred to text or speak face to face. And we also asked them why they had that preference. We asked who they thought it was appropriate to text. Oh, and we also asked them when they thought it was inappropriate to text. Finally, we asked if they had social media accounts and how often they posted to them.
Host	Well, it all sounds very interesting. Let's talk about your findings.

B 🔊 **2.04** **Now listen to the full interview and check (✓) the statements that are true.**

- ☐ 1 Millennials prefer digital communication, except at work.
- ☐ 2 Older people felt that text messages are **professional** enough for work.
- ☐ 3 All age groups reported using text messages to communicate with other family members at home.

2 VOCABULARY: Communicating online

A 🔊 **2.05** **Listen and say the words and phrases in the box. Which things can you identify in the picture? You can use your phone or a dictionary to help you.**

clickbait	geo-tag	hashtag
lifecaster	lurker	meme
newsfeed	podcaster	profile
status update	tag	timeline
trending topic		

B ▶ **Now go to page 147. Do the vocabulary exercises for 7.2.**

C **PAIR WORK** **Answer the questions.**
- What do you usually click on when you're looking at social media (photos, memes, trending topics)?
- What clickbait do you enjoy (animal videos, "Ten best" lists, celebrity gossip, personality quizzes, etc.)? What are some possible consequences of looking at clickbait?

Raquel Martinez is with Kara Lee and Kenny Waston at the Brunch House

At my favorite restaurant with some of my favorite people #SundayBrunch #Nomnomnom

👍 8

2 comments

😀

Hector you're such a lurker Lol. 😏

FIND IT

3 GRAMMAR: Reported questions

A **Choose the correct words to complete the rules. Use the sentences in the grammar box to help you.**

1 To report a question, **use / do not use** a question mark at the end of the sentence.

2 In a reported question, the subject comes **before / after** the verb. **Use / Do not use** the auxiliary *do/does* or *did*.

3 To report a *yes/no* question or a question about specific preferences, use *that / if*.

4 As with reported statements, verbs in reported questions change to the **present / past**.

Reported questions

Question	Reported question
"Do you prefer to communicate by text or face to face?" →	We asked them if they preferred to communicate by text or face to face.
"Who do you think it is appropriate to text?" →	We asked them who they thought it was appropriate to text.
"How often do you post to social media?" →	We asked them how often they posted to social media.

C ▶ **Now go to page 136. Do the grammar exercise for 7.2.**

D PAIR WORK **Think of some questions that you were asked recently. Report them and your answers to your partner. Check your accuracy.**

> A friend asked me if I wanted to go to the movies tonight. I said yes.

> A guy asked me where the tourist information office was. I didn't know!

✓ **ACCURACY** CHECK

When reporting questions, remember to use the word order of an affirmative sentence.

She asked what ~~did I do~~? ✗
She asked me what I did. ✓

4 SPEAKING

A PAIR WORK **Look at the questions. Choose two or three to ask and answer.**

■ Do you prefer to contact your coworkers by email, text message, or phone? Why? What about good friends or family?

■ Who do you text most frequently? How often do you see that person face to face?

■ Do you ever contact people via a social media message board? Why do you (or would you) use that kind of communication?

B PAIR WORK **Report the questions you were asked and the answers you gave to a different partner.**

> Maria asked me if I preferred to contact coworkers by email, text, or phone. I said that I liked to call people. It's much quicker.

1 FUNCTIONAL LANGUAGE

A ◀)) 2.06 **Look at the photos. What do you think the story behind them is? Read and listen to the conversations. Which conversation are the photos about? What do the stories have in common?**

◀)) **2.06 Audio script**

1 **A** **I heard that** David missed Andrew's wedding because he lost his phone. **Apparently,** he had all the info in there!

 B That's not what I heard. **Someone told me** that he "accidentally" overslept.

 A What? Who told you that?

 B Lauren. She asked him if he was upset about missing the wedding, and **he was like**, "Of course!" But **she was like**, "You don't look upset." Well, **turns out**, he was mad at Andrew and just didn't want to go.

2 **A** **You'll never believe what happened to** Marta! She was in a meeting at work, and **what happened was,** she fell asleep, right there in front of her boss!

 B You're kidding!

 A **The funny thing was**, she had been up all night preparing for that meeting!

 B What did her boss do?

 A At first he looked angry, but **in the end**, he laughed about it. Now it's a big joke around the office.

 B Really? I'm not sure that's any better!

B **Complete the chart with the bold expressions from the conversations.**

Recounting a conversation or story
I ¹_____ that (David missed the wedding).
Apparently, ...
Someone ²_____ me that ...
He was ³_____ , "(Of course.)"
Well, turns out, ...
You'll never ⁴_____ / guess what happened to ...
What ⁵_____ was, ...
The funny / strange ⁶_____ was, ...
In the ⁷_____ , (he laughed about it).

C ◀)) **2.07** **Complete the conversation using expressions from the chart. Listen and check. Then practice the conversation with a partner. Change some of the key information and do it again.**

A Barbara didn't come to work yesterday. She said she was sick.

B What? I sat with her on the bus. She wasn't sick.

A I know! Well, [1] _____ , she had an interview for another job.

B I thought so! She was wearing a very nice suit, and I'm [2] _____ , "You must have a job interview!" But she denied it.

A The [3] _____ was, the person who interviewed her called me to ask if she was a good employee! [4] _____ , Barbara wrote *me* down as a reference.

B Ha! I guess her secret isn't a secret anymore!

2 REAL WORLD STRATEGY

> **GETTING BACK ON TRACK**
>
> Sometimes you get interrupted or go off the topic when you're telling a story. You can use these expressions to get back on track.
>
> *As I was saying …*
> *Where was I? Oh yeah, …*
> *What was I saying?*
> *I lost my train of thought!*

A ◀)) **2.08** **Read the box about getting a conversation back on track. Then listen to another conversation. How does the listener interrupt? What does the speaker say to get them back on track?**

B **PAIR WORK** **Student A: Tell one of the stories from exercise 1A. Deal with any interruptions from Student B. Student B: Interrupt Student A's story two times. Student A: Get the conversation back on track. Switch roles and tell the other story.**

3 PRONUNCIATION FOCUS: Saying /s/ or /z/ at the end of a word

A ◀)) **2.09** **Listen and repeat. Focus on the sound of the bold letters.**

/s/ cour**se**   /z/ wa**s**

B ◀)) **2.10** **Listen. Write A for words with /s/. Write B for words with /z/.**

1	boss ___	3	bus ___	5	office ___
2	as ___	4	turns ___	6	lose ___

C **PAIR WORK** **Say the words in exercise 3B to your partner. Does your partner say the /s/ and /z/ sounds clearly?**

4 SPEAKING

A ▶ **Work in pairs. Student A: Go to page 157. Student B: Go to page 158. Read each story and act out a conversation for each one. Add details as you go.**

You'll never guess what happened! Gabrielle won first prize out of 20 candidates in the painting contest at school.

I know! And the funny thing is, she was the youngest one!

THE EMOJI CODE

1 READING

A **PAIR WORK** **Look at the pictures. In what contexts do you think the emoji and hashtag were used? In what situations do people generally use emojis, hashtags, and abbreviations (e.g. LOL)?**

> The #Paris might be to promote tourism.

B **READ FOR MAIN IDEAS** **Read the article from a student website and take notes. What is Dr. Patel's main argument? What is Prof. Yilmaz's main argument?**

IT'S A #WORLD

We all know that languages grow and change over time, new words are added to the dictionary, and old ones are removed. But what do we do with things like emojis and hashtags? They help us communicate, but are they language? We asked two professors for their opinions.

Arundhati Patel, professor of linguistics, says yes. Emojis are language because when you send a 😃 or a 😫, your message is immediately clear. Modern communication symbols are like body language – they help you express yourself.

Daniel Yilmaz, professor of English, disagrees. "There is a reason that the English language has more than 100,000 words in common use," he said. Real communication is complicated.

Symbols reduce our thoughts to simple personal opinions: #IhateMondays, 😣. Language, on the other hand, expresses deeper thoughts and complex ideas.

"But most of our daily communication needs are simple," Dr. Patel pointed out, "so why not satisfy them simply?" Prof. Yilmaz believes this "simplicity" is actually laziness. On most smartphones, for example, emoji menus come up automatically, so people take the easy road.

Dr. Patel and Prof. Yilmaz agree on one thing: hashtags are not language, they are politics. They unite people around ideas and attitudes.

So the debate continues. Do these modern communication symbols belong in the dictionary or not? Do we really have to decide? 😐

C **IDENTIFY OPINIONS** **Read the article again and answer the questions.**

1 Why does Dr. Patel think modern communication symbols are the same as language? What comparison does he make?

2 Why does Prof. Yilmaz claim emojis are not language? What does he think of emoji menus on smartphones?

3 What do the two professors agree on? What is their shared opinion?

FIND IT

D **THINK CRITICALLY** **PAIR WORK** **Do you think symbols help people communicate better? Why or why not? You can use your phone to find examples to support your opinion. For ideas, watch Alessandra's video.**

REAL STUDENT

Do you agree with Alessandra?

2 WRITING

A   Look at the two emails. In what context would you read each one? How do you know? What is the difference between them?

Email A

> Reply   Forward
>
> **To:** Patrick
> **From:** Melanie
> **Subject:** Final figures
>
> Hi Patrick,
>
> How's things? Strange day at the office. Very boring meeting! – 😴 then big meal 🍔. But can meet 2:30ish?? Have to be at the docs at 4 😖
>
> Ok with you??? Let me know when you get a sec.
>
> Speak soon!
>
> 😘
>
> Melanie

Email B

> Reply   Forward
>
> **To:** Patrick
> **From:** Melanie
> **Subject:** Final figures
>
> Dear Patrick,
>
> I'm writing to see if we can find a time to meet later today. We need to go over the final figures together. I have a meeting all morning, and I'm meeting a client for lunch. I can meet around 2:30, but I'll need to leave at 4 for a doctor's appointment.
>
> Does that time suit you? If not, could you suggest another time?
>
> Looking forward to speaking with you,
>
> Melanie

B   **WRITING SKILL** Identify the elements of informal register in email A and formal register in email B. How do the emojis change the register?

C   Find the formal equivalents in email B for these informal phrases in email A.

Informal	Formal
Very boring meeting!	I have a meeting all morning.
OK with you???	
Speak soon!	

D   GROUP WORK Think of other information that you could include in email B (formal). Check the elements that would be appropriate. Which of them would be appropriate for an informal email, too?

a Gossip ☐
b Your health ☐
c Changes at work ☐
d Scheduling meetings ☐
e Free time – weekend plans ☐
f Question about a work problem ☐

 **WRITE IT**

E   Write two short emails – one formal message to a coworker and one informal message to a friend. In both messages, update the person on what you have been doing at work or in your free time and include plans to meet. Be sure to use different registers in the two messages. Write a maximum of 100 words in each email.

F   PAIR WORK Read your emails. Identify different elements of formal and informal register. Are the appropriate words and phrases used in each message?

7.5

TIME TO SPEAK
Online Communication Survey

A **PREPARE** Look at the pictures. How are these people using their smartphones? What are some other ways to use a smartphone? How many of the uses are related to communicating with someone?

B **DISCUSS** With a partner, read the survey about online communication and add some questions of your own. Then answer all of the questions and take notes on your answers.

> 1 How many social media accounts do you have? What do you use each one for?
> 2 How many text messages do you write every day? Who to?
> 3 How many calls do you make every day? Who to?
> 4 How do you keep up with the news? Which source do you use most? Why?
> 5 _____
> 6 _____
> 7 _____

C **PRESENT** Report your results to the class and listen to the other results. Then, with your partner, draw conclusions about the full results of the survey.

D **AGREE** Share your conclusions with the class. Did everyone reach the same or similar conclusions? Discuss the points you disagree on.

⟩⟩ *To check your progress, go to page 155.* ⟩⟩

USEFUL PHRASES

PREPARE
To me, these images mean …
I think they represent …

DISCUSS
I think we should ask about …
So, which social media sites … ?
My favorite news source is … because …

PRESENT
The results of this survey clearly show …
From this survey, we can conclude …
The results don't give us enough information on …

UNIT OBJECTIVES:

- talk about different work lifestyles
- talk about wishes and regrets
- talking through options to reach a decision
- write a comment about a podcast
- plan and discuss a digital detox weekend for your class

LIFESTYLES

8

START SPEAKING

A   Look at the people in the picture. What words would you use to describe them? What do you think their lifestyle is like?

B   Think about your work life (current or future). Will your job determine what kind of lifestyle you have, or will you choose a job that matches the lifestyle you want? For ideas, watch Maryne's video.

REAL STUDENT

Are your answers the same as Maryne's?

THE PERFECT JOB?

1 LANGUAGE IN CONTEXT

A Look at the picture and its caption in the post below. What job is the ad for? Read the full post. Is the writer interested in applying for the job? Why or why not?

If you saw this job ad on your timeline, would you click to find out more? I did, along with 300,000 other people!

The island of Maatsuyker in Tasmania is looking for two temporary caretakers to live on the island for six months each. No television or internet access. The work is not very stressful, as the lighthouse runs automatically. The caretaker's job is basically to report on data from the weather station, so it's not a tough job. It rains a lot, but the views and the wildlife are amazing. Everybody who visits falls in love with the island.

Island seeks lighthouse caretaker for six months.
Click here to apply!

What was your first reaction? Would you enjoy being cut off from the rest of the world for six months? Does that sound like your dream job?

I'm not so sure I could do it! Maybe if I was single and didn't have kids I might do it. But with a family, I need a permanent job – preferably one that's high-paying! What about you? If you were free to do it, would you apply for this job?

FIND IT

B **PAIR WORK** Do you think you could do the job described in the ad? Why or why not? You can use your phones to find out more about the island before you answer.

2 VOCABULARY: Describing jobs

FIND IT

A 🔊 **2.11** **PAIR WORK** Listen and say the words in the box. Which ones are in the post? Do they have a positive or negative meaning? What about the other words? Look them up in a dictionary or on your phone if needed.

challenging	desk job	dream job	freelance	full-time
government job	high-paying	main job	part-time	permanent
second job	stressful	temporary	tiring	tough

B Which words in the box are useful to give a factual description of a job? <u>Underline</u> them. Which words express an opinion? (Circle) them.

C ▶ Now go to page 148. Do the vocabulary exercises for 8.1.

D **PAIR WORK** Describe the jobs in the box using the descriptions in exercise A.

babysitter	doctor	firefighter
lifeguard	fashion designer	sales assistant

> *Well, being a babysitter is probably a part-time job, and it isn't very high-paying, but it is very challenging.*

3 GRAMMAR: Present unreal conditionals

A **Read the sentences in the grammar box. Then complete the rules.**

Present unreal conditionals

If you **saw** this ad on your timeline, **would** you **click** to find out more?

If you **were** free to do it, **would** you **apply** for this job?

If I **was** single and **didn't have** kids and **wanted** to write a book or something, I **might do** it.

REGISTER CHECK

In formal language, use *were* for all subjects, including 1st and 3rd person.

If I were selected, I would devote myself to it.

In informal language, you can use *was* for 1st and 3rd person subjects.

If I / she was feeling better, I / she would go.

1 The sentences refer to **a real / an imagined** situation.

2 Look at the **bold** verbs. The verb form that follows *if* is **simple present / simple past**. It **refers / doesn't refer** to a past situation.

B ▶ **Now go to page 136. Look at the grammar chart and do the grammar exercise for 8.1.**

C PAIR WORK **Complete the questions with the correct form of the verb in parentheses ( ). Ask and answer the questions with your partner.**

1 If you _____ (can do) any job in the world, what job _____ you _____ (choose)? Why?

2 _____ you _____ (consider) doing a job you loved if you _____ (not be) paid well? Why or why not?

3 What _____ you _____ (do) with your free time if you _____ (not have to) work?

4 SPEAKING

A **Read about two more jobs. How are they similar to the lighthouse caretaker job?**

Resort caretaker: In the summer we work with the tourists, but in the winter, it's just my wife and me. It snows a lot and the mountains are beautiful. There's a lot of work to do maintaining all the buildings, but there's plenty of free time, too. And the wildlife is fantastic! Last winter we had bears come to visit us. That was awesome!

Drone pilot: I'm working with a team to help study seabirds. Using drones, I get amazing pictures of the birds in their nests with their babies. The scientists who run the project come about once a month, but mostly we have the island to ourselves. Our housing and food are pretty basic, but I'm learning a lot, and getting college credit!

B PAIR WORK **If you had to choose one of the three jobs in this lesson, which one would you choose? Why? What do you think daily life would be like?**

If I was the resort caretaker, I'd have a lot of free time to do all kinds of snow sports.

If a drone pilot was a high-paying job, I'd pick that one.

8.2 FINDING A BALANCE

1 LANGUAGE IN CONTEXT

A 🔊 **2.12** Listen to a psychologist discussing the problem of finding the right work/life balance. What solution does she suggest?

B 🔊 **2.12** Listen again and read the script. Find at least three examples of things we associate with work and three things we associate with free time.

> 🔊 **2.12 Audio script**
>
> Have you ever said, "I wish I didn't have to work such long hours?" Whether you're an executive with one meeting after another, a full-time student attending **lectures** and **seminars**, or a parent who works the late **shift**, the problem is always the same – How can I have a life with such a **busy schedule**?
>
> I hear it all the time: I wish I had more time for **family life**, I wish I hadn't promised to work this weekend, I wish I could take some **time off**, I wish I had more **me time**! There are hundreds of articles out there about how to balance work and life, but we need to stop seeing work and life as two opposing forces that we have to balance. We need to think about how to *combine* them.
>
> Take this example: a client of mine now schedules **downtime** into his working day. He takes a short walk, has a relaxing lunch with a friend, or goes home a little early to spend time with the kids. Then, after they're asleep, he sits down and writes that report he needs for tomorrow.
>
> Making your job and your life work together is a great way to enjoy them both.

C PAIR WORK Do you think it's a good idea to combine your work or school life with your social life? Why or why not?

2 VOCABULARY: Talking about work/life balance

FIND IT

A 🔊 **2.13** PAIR WORK Listen and say the words and phrases in the box. Discuss where they should go in the Venn diagram. You can use your phone or a dictionary to help you.

always connected	assignments	busy schedule	chilling out	commitments
downtime	family life	lectures	me time	office hours
seminars	shift	social life	time off	9-to-5

> Commitments: I guess that could be work, school, or home life. Let's put it in the middle.

work/school   commitments   home life

B ▶ Now go to page 148. Do the vocabulary exercises for 8.2.

C GROUP WORK Do you feel you have a busy schedule? Do you get enough downtime? Is your downtime also "me time"?

3 GRAMMAR: *I wish*

A **Choose the correct words to complete the rules. Use the sentences in the grammar box to help you.**

1 "*I wish*" sentences express that you want things to **stay the same / be different**.

2 The main verb of the sentence **stays in the same tense / changes tense**. The modal "*can*" **stays the same / changes to** *could*.

3 Affirmative statements **change to negative / stay affirmative**.

4 Negative statements **change to affirmative / stay negative**.

I wish

I **have to** work long hours.	→	I wish I **didn't have to** work such long hours.
I **don't have** much free time.	→	I wish I **had** more free time.
I **can't take** any time off next week.	→	I wish I **could take** some time off next week.
I **promised** to work this weekend.	→	I wish I **hadn't promised** to work this weekend.

B  **Now go to page 137. Look at the grammar chart and do the grammar exercise for 8.2.**

C PAIR WORK **Complete the wishes so that they are true for you. Review them with a partner and check your accuracy.**

1 I wish I knew _____

2 I wish I could _____

3 I wish I wasn't/weren't _____

4 I wish I didn't have to _____

5 I wish I hadn't _____

6 I wish I had _____

✓ ACCURACY CHECK

Don't confuse *wish* and *hope*. Use *hope* to talk about something you want to happen in the future.
I hope you'll be there on Saturday.

Use *wish* to talk about a situation you can't change.
I wish you could come on Saturday, but I know you have to work.

4 SPEAKING

A PAIR WORK **Look at the list of wishes. Which do you think are the most common? Why?**

I wish I had gone to a different college.
I wish I had studied harder in high school.
I wish I could play a musical instrument.
I wish I could get a different job.

I wish I could travel more.
I wish I was younger.
I wish I was older.

B PAIR WORK **Think of three more common wishes. Who might have them? Compare your ideas with other students. For ideas, watch Seung Geyong's video.**

 REAL STUDENT

 Are any of your wishes the same as Seung Geyong's?

8.3 I WOULDN'T DO THAT!

1 FUNCTIONAL LANGUAGE

A 🔊 **2.14** **Laura has a meeting on Saturday morning but she doesn't want to go. Listen to Laura and her mother discussing Laura's options. What do you think Laura decides to do?**

🔊 **2.14 Audio script**

A Great! My boss just scheduled a meeting for Saturday. It's going to take so long to get there and get back, you know, with the weekend train schedule.

B Too bad, Laura. **Is there any way you can** get out of it?

A Well, I guess I could stay at a hotel Friday night, but that's expensive.

B Well, it's a possibility, but it isn't ideal. **Have you tried talking** to your boss? **If I were in your shoes,** I'd explain the situation and offer an alternative. I mean, **it can't hurt,** right?

A I guess I could, but what alternative?

B Well, **you might want to** suggest meeting up on Monday morning to catch up, or **maybe you could** offer to attend remotely instead? **I'd try that if I were you.**

A Yeah, I guess I could ask him if I could attend by phone or Skype.

B **It wouldn't hurt** to ask. I mean, **you've got nothing to lose.**

B Complete the chart with the **bold** expressions from the conversation.

Talking through options
Is there any ¹_____ you can (get out of it)?
Have you ²_____ (talking to him)?
If I were in your ³_____, I'd (explain the situation).
You might ⁴_____ to (suggest meeting on Monday).
Maybe you ⁵_____ (offer to attend remotely).

Encouraging actions
It can't ⁶_____.
I'd (try that) if I ⁷_____ you.
It wouldn't ⁸_____ (to ask).
You've got nothing to ⁹_____.

INSIDER ENGLISH

You can use I guess to consider suggestions.
I guess I could.
I guess it wouldn't hurt.

C 🔊 **2.15** **PAIR WORK** **Complete the conversation with phrases from the chart. Listen and check your answers. Then practice the conversation.**

A I really don't want to go out to dinner tonight. I'm so tired, but I promised Ellen.

B ¹_____ suggesting another time?

A Yes, but she's leaving for school tomorrow. I'd really like to see her before she goes.

B Well, you might ²_____ ask her to meet up earlier. Or maybe you ³_____ invite her over to your place instead? I'd try that ⁴_____ I were you.

A Yeah, that's a great idea. I'll text her now. Thanks!

2 REAL WORLD STRATEGY

A 🔊 **2.16** **Listen to two short conversations. What's the situation in each?**

> **OFFERING A WARNING**
>
> Sometimes you want to encourage someone *not* to do something.
>
> | *You don't want to do that!*
> | *I wouldn't do that if I were you.*
> | *You might not want to do that.*
> | *I'd avoid that if I were you.*

B 🔊 **2.16** **Read the information about warnings in the box and then listen again. What warning is offered in each conversation? What advice is given?**

C PAIR WORK **Read each statement and discuss why it's a bad idea. What warning would you give? What would you suggest instead?**

1 "I need to cancel a meeting with my boss for this morning. I think I'm going to tell him I'm sick."

2 "I really don't want to go to Dale's birthday party tonight. I think I just won't go."

3 "I really should study tonight. I did really bad on the last test. But I think I'll go to Ben's party instead.

3 PRONUNCIATION FOCUS: Saying the vowel sounds /ɜ/ and /u/

A 🔊 **2.17** **Listen and repeat the two different vowel sounds.**

/ɜ/ h**ur**t   It wouldn't hurt to ask.   /u/ l**o**se   You have nothing to lose.

B 🔊 **2.18** **Listen. Write A for words with /ɜ/. Write B for words with /u/.**

1	sch**e**dule ___	3	**you** ___	5	b**ir**thday ___
2	**a**lternative ___	4	sch**oo**l ___	6	f**ew** ___

C 🔊 **2.19** PAIR WORK **Listen to the conversations. Then practice with a partner.**

1 **A** What are **you** doing for your b**ir**thday?
  B Not much. I have to go to sch**oo**l.

2 **A** This r**oo**m is a little small. Should we ask for a nicer one?
  B It can't h**ur**t to ask. We've got nothing to l**o**se.

4 SPEAKING

A **Choose one of the topics and think of a situation where someone might have many options to consider. Make notes about different options and the kind of advice you could offer.**

family	health	money	relationships	studies	work

Health: someone wants to get in shape

Advice: start swimming, running, bicycling; do yoga, zumba; take an exercise class

B PAIR WORK **Use your notes to act out the situation. Decide who is going to ask for advice and who is going to give it. Try to include a warning as well. Then switch roles.**

DIGITAL DETOX

1 LISTENING

A **PAIR WORK** Look at the pictures. What are the main differences between the two situations? Which one do you think shows a more positive use of mobile technology? Why?

B 🔊 2.20 **LISTEN FOR ATTITUDE** Listen to an extract from a podcast about mobile technology. What is a "digital detox"? How do the two speakers, Tim and Kayla, feel about the idea? Would you ever consider a digital detox?

C 🔊 2.20 **PAIR WORK** Read the extracts. Who do you think said each one? Write *T* (Tim) or *K* (Kayla). How do you know? Listen again to check your answers.

1 I love my phone too much! _____

2 I would never do that, not for a million dollars! _____

3 You don't always have to share everything. _____

4 What's wrong with sharing? _____

5 It's so important that we know what's going on in the world. _____

6 I could be doing something better. _____

7 I am very happy with my 24/7, always connected life. _____

> **INSIDER** ENGLISH
>
> The phrase *not for a million dollars* is often used to show strong dislike for an idea.
>
> *I'd never give up my phone – not for a million dollars!*

D **CRITICAL THINKING** Who do you agree with more? Do you think people need to learn how to control their use of digital devices? Do you think a digital detox is the best way? Can you think of other ways?

2 PRONUNCIATION: Listening for emphasis

A 🔊 2.21 Listen to the extracts from the podcast. Focus on how the speaker says the **bold** words.

1 A digital detox, me? Are you kidding? No way, I love my phone **way** too much.

2 I'm glad you stepped up, Tim, because I would **never** do that!

3 We did it in this cabin out in the forest, and it was **really** quiet and relaxing.

B **Choose the correct words to complete the sentence.**

When a speaker wants to add emphasis to an idea, they often say the word *higher / stronger* and *shorter / longer.*

3 WRITING

A **Read the two comments that were left on the podcast. Which one was written by the podcast host and which one by a listener? How do you know?**

Comments   Sign out   Account

1 I really enjoyed listening to this week's podcast. Good for you, Tim, trying a digital detox! It's something I've thought about. If I had the time, I'd do it. There was one thing in particular that interested me in your conversation, when you were talking about sharing photos. It made me think of how I use social media to keep in touch with friends and family that I don't get to see that often. I don't think I'd be as good at keeping in touch if I didn't have social media. Do you think social media might actually help us have better social relationships? And, as Kayla said, it is important to keep up with what is going on in the world. Looking forward to hearing your opinion!

⛓ Share   👍 Like   💬 Comment

2 Hi there. Thanks for leaving your comment. That's a really interesting question, and I'm really not sure how to answer it. You point out that social media makes it easier to keep in contact with friends and family. Personally, I think face-to-face contact with people is always better, and nothing beats spending time with someone. But if they live in another city or country or something, then I guess maybe smartphones and social media do help a lot. I wonder what other people have to say about that!

⛓ Share   👍 Like   💬 Comment

B **WRITING SKILL** **Look at the two comments again. <u>Underline</u> the phrases that reference another person's statement or opinion.**

C **PAIR WORK** **Read the comments again. Do you think smartphones help us have better social relationships? Why or why not?**

 **WRITE IT**

D **Write a response to the two comments. Remember to 1) refer back to both the question and the answer, 2) make a positive reference to the podcast, and 3) invite other opinions on the topic.**

TIME TO SPEAK
Planning a digital detox

A **DISCUSS** As a class, discuss this question: If you had to live without your phone for a week, how would that affect your day-to-day life? Think of all the things you usually do with your phone. What would you miss the most?

B You and a partner are going to arrange a digital detox weekend for your class. Think of the answers your classmates gave. Who do you think would suffer the most from the detox? Why?

C A TV company is going to sponsor your weekend and make a documentary about the experience. Think about these things:

- Where could you hold the detox? Think of places in or near your city.
- What facilities would you need? Think of alternatives to digital devices, for example, a gym or a library.
- What activities would you like to offer? How could you help people when they're missing their phones? Think of a variety of different activities for both daytime and evening hours.

There are some big houses by the beach. We'd need lots of bedrooms but just one kitchen. A gym would be great, and if we had a library, people could still read, just not on their tablets. Our experience is going to be filmed, so we should have some conflicts too, for drama, like some sports activities.

D **DECIDE** Create a plan for the weekend. Include this information:

- what time the program starts on Friday and ends on Sunday
- morning, afternoon, and evening activity choices for the full three days

E **PRESENT** Present your program to the class. Answer any questions from the audience.

F **AGREE** Which pair of students has planned the best program? Why do you think so?

To check your progress, go to page 155.

USEFUL PHRASES

DISCUSS
If I had to …, I think I'd …
I'd really miss …
If we held the detox [place], then people might …

DECIDE
I think we should / could …
Why don't we … ?
What about … ?

PRESENT
We decided / thought that …
We chose to …
We want to / We'd like to …

- talk about rules and regulations in your everyday life
- discuss rules and regulations in the past
- make generalizations
- write a letter of complaint
- discuss improvements to your town

YES, YOU CAN!

9

START SPEAKING

A   Look at the signs. What does the original sign mean? Describe how it was changed. Do you think this is funny? Why or why not?

B   Think of another way the sign could be altered and draw it. Compare your design with the rest of the class. Who has the best one?

C   What interesting graffiti or street art can you see in or around your neighborhood? For ideas, watch Seung Geyong's video.

REAL STUDENT

Have you ever seen something similar?

READING THE SIGNS

1 LANGUAGE IN CONTEXT

A 🔊 **2.22** **PAIR WORK** **Look at the signs. What do you think they mean? Listen to two people discussing some of the signs. Check (✓) the ones they mention. Were you right about their meanings?**

🔊 **2.22 Audio script**

Bart   So many signs everywhere! *No parking, No skateboards, No entry …*

Luisi   There's one saying you aren't supposed to bring your pets inside. And there, you *are* allowed to bring your guide dog inside.

Bart   And look there! You're required to wear a hard hat on the **construction site**.

Luisi   That makes sense, but I've noticed some strange ones recently. Outside the **arts center** one said you aren't allowed to wear a hoodie inside! I think it's so someone can't hide their face – the security cameras should be able to see you clearly.

Bart   Oh, I get it. I saw a cool sign at **city hall**, just outside the **courthouse**. It's a pair of hands and a speech bubble. It means that you may request a sign language interpreter if you need one.

Luisi   Hey, that *is* cool! Oh! I saw a really strange one on the **boardwalk** – it was a wheelchair underwater!

Bart   A wheelchair underwater? I don't get it.

Luisi   It means there's no access for wheelchairs. Like, it's not physically possible for wheelchairs to get to the beach.

Bart   Oh. That's a shame.

2 VOCABULARY: Talking about places

FIND IT

A 🔊 **2.23** **PAIR WORK** **Listen and say the words in the box. Look up the ones you don't know on your phone or in a dictionary. Which sign(s) from exercise 1A would you expect to see in each place?**

arts center	boardwalk	city hall	consulate
construction site	courthouse	highway rest stop	laboratory
playground	public space	residential area	toll plaza

INSIDER ENGLISH

I get it or *I don't get it* means that you do or don't understand something.

What? I don't get it.

B ▶ **Now go to page 149. Do the vocabulary exercises for 9.1.**

C **PAIR WORK** **What other signs do you see around you every day? Where do you see them? Do people generally obey these signs? Are there any signs that people sometimes ignore?**

> There are "no cell phones" signs in the movie theater. I wish more people obeyed them!

3 GRAMMAR: Prohibition, permission, obligation (present)

Prohibition, permission, obligation (present)	
Prohibition	You **may not** skateboard here.
	You **aren't allowed to** wear a hoodie.
	You **aren't supposed to** bring your pets inside.
Permission	You **are allowed to** bring in your guide dog.
	You **may** request an interpreter.
Obligation	The cameras **should** be able to see you.
	You**'re required to** wear a hard hat.
	You**'re supposed to** ring the bell for service.

A   Read the sentences in the grammar box. Then (circle) all the correct answers to complete the rules.

1   Prohibition can also be expressed with …

   a *can't*　　　　**b** *must not*　　　　**c** *won't*

2   Permission can also be expressed with …

   a *want to*　　　**b** *would like to*　　**c** *can*

3   Obligation or necessity can also be expressed with …

   a *(don't) need to*　**b** *(don't) have to*　**c** *shouldn't*

B   ▶ **Now go to page 137. Look at the grammar chart and do the grammar exercise for 9.1.**

C   GROUP WORK   **Choose one of the places in the box or another place that everyone knows. Think of at least five rules for that place. Use different structures from the grammar box in your rules.**

   airport terminal   campground   hospital   school   theater

D   **Read your rules to the class. Can anyone guess which place it is?**

4 SPEAKING

A   GROUP WORK   **Discuss the questions.**

   ■ What rules and regulations do you have to follow at work or school? In your house or apartment?

   ■ Which rules would you like to change or get rid of completely? Why?

   ■ What new rules would you like to introduce? Why?

B   GROUP WORK   **Choose two of the rules you'd like to introduce (from the previous exercise) and draw a sign to illustrate them. Show them to the class. Can they guess what your rules are?**

> My new rule is "no one is allowed to chew gum in the study area."

1 LANGUAGE IN CONTEXT

A Look at the pictures. What can you see in each one? What traffic rules are represented? Imagine driving in a city where there were no traffic rules. What would happen?

B Read this article about William Eno. What's the connection with the pictures above?

STOP and GO

Before cars were invented, horse-drawn carriages were allowed to circulate freely. There were no signs to **control** traffic and no speed **limits**. As cars started to appear on the streets, rules that would **permit** traffic to flow safely were desperately needed.

In 1903, William Eno published "Rules for Driving" – the first official traffic code. Drivers had to drive on the right, they were supposed to show other drivers when they wanted to turn, and they were **prohibited** from parking on the left. His greatest innovations were the traffic circle and one-way streets, which **obliged** all traffic to travel in the same direction. He also helped introduce crosswalks to protect pedestrians. At the same time, new laws **required** vehicles to be **registered** and have license plates and also **banned** drivers under sixteen, though drivers did not have to take a driving test until 1934.

The most curious thing about Eno, the father of road safety, was that he never learned to drive a car!

GLOSSARY
license plate (*n*) a sign on a car that shows its registration number

C Read the article again. Check (✓) the statements that you can infer from the text. Find information in the text to support your answers and <u>underline</u> it.

- [ ] 1 Before cars, there were very few problems with traffic in big cities like New York.
- [ ] 2 There was no traffic code before cars.
- [ ] 3 Eno's "Rules for Driving" included more than just rules for drivers.
- [ ] 4 Eno was not physically able to drive a car.

2 VOCABULARY: Talking about rules

A 🔊 **2.24** **Complete the chart. What idea do the words express? Write *M* (must), *A* (allowed), *N* (not allowed), or *R* (rules apply). Listen and check.**

verb	noun	meaning	verb	noun	meaning
	ban			permission	
control		R		prohibition	
limit			register		
	obligation			requirement	

B ▶ **Now go to page 149. Do the vocabulary exercises for 9.2.**

C GROUP WORK **What are three problems caused by traffic where you live? Suggest solutions for each of the problems. For ideas, watch Nicolle's video.**

REAL STUDENT

Do you agree with Nicolle?

3 GRAMMAR: Prohibition, permission, obligation (past)

A **Complete the sets. Use the sentences in the grammar box to help you. Then decide which set each example sentence belongs to: *A*, *B*, or *C*.**

A To express prohibition in the past: *couldn't,* _____

B To express permission in the past: *could,* _____

C To express obligation in the past: *had to,* _____

> **Prohibition, permission, obligation (past)**
>
> Carriages **were allowed to** circulate freely before 1903.   B
> Eno's rules said that drivers **had to** drive on the right.   ___
> They **were not allowed to** stop in the middle of the street. ___
> Pedestrians **were required to** cross at the crosswalk. ___

B ▶ **Now go to page 138. Look at the grammar chart and do the grammar exercise for 9.2.**

C GROUP WORK **Write three rules from your childhood. Use three different structures from the grammar box, and check your accuracy. Read your rules to the group. Whose parents were the strictest?**

 ACCURACY CHECK

Prohibition and permission are usually expressed in the passive because the person / authority responsible for the law is known and doesn't need to be named.

City regulations allow cars to park here. (correct, but authority is known)
Cars are allowed to park here.

4 SPEAKING

A GROUP WORK **Read the laws. Three of them were real laws in the past. Which is the fake law? Why do you think people passed the real laws?**

1 You couldn't drink soda on Sunday.

2 All men were required to grow beards.

3 Female school teachers were not allowed to get married.

4 Only people who weighed more than 100 pounds (45 kilograms) could vote in elections.

FIND IT

B **Do you know any old laws from your country? Go online and find out if they are still laws. Find some strange laws from other countries, too.**

9.3 TO TIP OR NOT TO TIP?

1 FUNCTIONAL LANGUAGE

A ◀)) **2.25** [PAIR WORK] **Look at the picture. Where is the person? How much money do you think they're giving? Listen to Charlie and Júlia talking about tipping in the U.S. Is it similar in your country?**

◀)) 2.25 Audio script

A I'll pick up the check if you leave the tip, Júlia.

B OK, thanks, Charlie. But how much should I leave?

A Well, **generally speaking** we leave 15–20%.

B Really? That much? In Brazil, people don't **tend to** tip nearly as much as that. Oh! Should I tip in cafés as well, and fast food places?

A If there's no table service, we **generally** don't tip, but there may be a jar on the counter for you to drop some coins into if you want.

B I've seen that in Brazil, too. What about taxi drivers? Are you required to tip them?

A Required? No, not really, but, **on average**, people tip 5–10% of the fare.

B Ten per cent! Wow, all these tips must get expensive!

A Well, you know, **on the whole,** service jobs don't pay well, so people in the service industry really rely on tips to make a living.

B **Complete the chart with the bold expressions from the conversation.**

Making generalizations
Generally [1] _____ , (we leave 15–20%).
People don't [2] _____ to (tip so much).
We [3] _____ (don't tip in fast food places).
On [4] _____ , (people tip 5–10%).
On the [5] _____ , (service jobs don't pay well).

> **!** Use *on average* with a number or quantity.
>
> *On average*, people tip drivers 5–10% of the fare.

C **Complete the generalizations using a phrase from the chart. Are they true in your country?**

1 _____ speaking, we don't really give that many tips.

2 People _____ to tip more in nicer restaurants.

3 _____ , service industry workers don't depend on tips.

4 People _____ don't tip taxi drivers unless it's a long journey.

5 _____ , people tip around 10% in restaurants.

2 REAL WORLD STRATEGY

A 🔊 2.26 Listen to Júlia and Charlie discussing two other cultural differences. What are they?

> **CONTRASTING INFORMATION**
>
> When you want to contrast cultural information, you can use several different expressions.
>
> *We don't tip nearly as much as that.*
> *Really? We don't do that where I come from.*
> *We don't do it that way in my country.*
> *We do things differently back home.*
> *We handle tipping differently where I come from.*
> *That's not how we do / say it in (Portuguese).*

B 🔊 2.26 Read the information on contrasting information in the box and listen again. What phrase does Júlia use to contrast their customs each time?

C PAIR WORK Look at these common customs in the U.S. Are they the same in your country?
  1 The waiter refills your coffee cup at no extra charge.
  2 The national anthem (national song) is played before every professional sporting event or game.
  3 On an escalator, people stand on the right side and walk on the left side.

3 PRONUNCIATION FOCUS: Saying /d/ at the beginning of a word

A 🔊 2.27 Listen and repeat. Focus on the /d/ sounds.
  1 We generally **d**on't tip.   2 We **d**o things **d**ifferently.

B 🔊 2.28 Listen. Who says the /d/ sound? Write A or B.
  1 drop ____   3 depend ____   5 difficult ____
  2 different ____   4 do ____   6 deep ____

C PAIR WORK Say the words in exercise 3B to your partner. Does your partner say the /d/ sound clearly?

4 SPEAKING

A Think about a time when you visited a new town or country. In what ways were things different there?

B PAIR WORK Tell your partner about your impressions. React to your partner's impressions with surprise when appropriate.

> *On the whole, people wear more colorful clothes than we wear back home.*

THE STORY OF THE RAMP

1 READING

A **READ FOR GIST** Look at the picture in the article. What is the red structure? In what ways is it useful? Read the article to check your answers. Then choose the best title for the article. Why is it the best?

a Ed Roberts and the independent living movement

b A short history of wheelchair ramps

c Student life at the University of California

Ed Roberts was the first student with significant disabilities to be allowed to attend The University of California at Berkeley. It was the 1960s, and there was no access for wheelchairs on campus. Roberts and other disability activists fought for access and even built their own ramps in the middle of the night so that wheelchair users could enter university buildings independently.

Thanks to the work of Roberts and other disability activists, the first Center for Independent Living was founded in Berkeley in 1972. It offered support for disabled students, and was staffed by people with disabilities who had personal experience of fighting for equal access. There are now more than 400 centers around the United States.

Over the next 20 years, the independent living movement grew in number and strength. In 1990, the Americans with Disabilities Act was passed. This law requires all businesses and institutions to provide access to wheelchairs, which opened up a world of new opportunities. After Robert's death in 1995, a nonprofit organization called the Ed Roberts Campus was founded in his memory. The Campus facilities provide community meeting rooms, offices for non-profit organizations, and many other community focused services. One of its most recognizable features is the famous red ramp.

There are still battles to be won, however. Wheelchair users are still fighting for their right to equal access. A ramp may seem like a very simple thing, but it's a powerful tool in supporting independent living.

B **PAIR WORK** **RECALL KEY INFORMATION** Before you read the article again, look at the numbers and dates in the box. Can you remember what they referred to? Check your answers in the article.

| 1960s | 1972 | 400 | 1990 | 1995 |

C **GROUP WORK** **THINK CRITICALLY** Think about public spaces where you live. Can wheelchairs access them easily? Is access required by law? Who do you think should pay for providing wheelchair access in shops: the business, the local authorities, charities or someone else? Why?

2 WRITING

A Read this message that a customer left for a restaurant owner on their website. What was the problem? What does the customer want to do? Why?

Your message:

Last week I visited your restaurant. It was the first time I'd visited, and I was excited about going. I use a wheelchair, so building access is always a worry and going anywhere new means doing some research first. But things looked good. Fortunately, your website showed a ramp leading up into your entrance so I was confident I could get in.

And, in fact, I got up the ramp and entered the front door without any trouble. Disappointingly, inside there's a step down to the dining room. It's just one step, but it may as well have been a wall. Embarrassingly, I had to ask your staff for help, and soon all eyes in the restaurant were on me. Happily, from then on everything was wonderful. We enjoyed a delicious meal and great service.

I imagine you're aware that there's a law that requires your business to provide access to wheelchair users. I represent an association that helps businesses make simple changes so that they meet the requirements of the law. I'd be happy to meet you at your restaurant to go over some ways to make your business more accessible to people like me.

I look forward to your reply.

Send

REGISTER CHECK

When writing to a business or a person about a problem, you can end with *"I look forward to your reply"* to show that you expect action to be taken.

B **WRITING SKILL** Read the message again. What was the writer happy with at the restaurant? What was he not happy about? Underline four adverbs that communicate the writer's attitude.

C Which adverbs from the box below can replace the adverbs you underlined in the message. More than one answer may be possible.

amazingly   luckily   sadly   surprisingly   unfortunately   unluckily

 **WRITE IT**

D Think of a time when you were unhappy with a product or service, and write your own message to register a complaint in about 100 words. Use some of the words from exercises B and C to show your attitude.

E PAIR WORK Read each other's messages. What do you think the receiver will do – ignore it, apologize, or try to make it right? Why?

TIME TO SPEAK
Making a difference

A **DISCUSS** Look at the pictures. What problems are the different people facing? What types of problems might they face where you live? Think of access to buildings, facilities in public spaces, etc.

B Work in pairs or small groups. Look at the groups of people below and think of other groups with common interests and issues. Discuss the things they might want to do (use public transportation, access public spaces, go shopping, etc.) and think of three problems they might face in your neighborhood.

- families with young children
- wheelchair users
- dog owners

C Choose a group to focus on. Discuss possible solutions to the three problems you identified. What laws or rules could be introduced to help them? What facilities could be offered? What other solutions might there be?

D **PRESENT** Present to the class both the problems you identified for the group of people you selected and your solutions to those problems.

E **AGREE** Vote on the most ambitious, the most practical, and the most imaginative solutions.

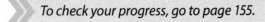 To check your progress, go to page 155.

USEFUL PHRASES

 DISCUSS
They might have problems getting …
They may not be able to …
They may not be allowed to ….
Local businesses could …

Local authorities should …
It'd be a good idea to …
If there were enough space, they could …

 PRESENT
We discussed …
We decided that …
We suggest that …

REVIEW 3 (UNITS 7–9)

1 VOCABULARY

A Complete the chart with the words and phrases below. Then write a category for each group.

arts center	ban	boardwalk	congratulate	criticize
downtime	high-paying	lectures	oblige	persuade
playground	prohibit	shift	temporary	time off

gossip	part-time	assignments	city hall	permit
comment	9-to-5	busy schedule	courthouse	require

B Think of at least two more words or phrases for each group.

2 GRAMMAR

A Choose the correct words to complete the conversation.

A I'm so tired. I wish I ¹can / could go away for the weekend.

B Why don't you? What about your brother's place? If my brother ²has / had a cabin in the mountains, ³I'd go / I went there every weekend.

A I thought of that. I asked my brother if he ⁴invited / had invited anyone for the weekend.

B What did he say?

A He said he ⁵wasn't / hadn't sure, and then he mentioned that his wife ⁶invites / had invited her parents over.

B Too bad. Hey, why don't we go camping at South River Park?

A Now, that's an idea. Do you know if dogs ⁷allowed / are allowed in the park?

B Not anymore. Sorry, but Buddy ⁸may not / couldn't come along.

B PAIR WORK What is something you wish you could do this coming weekend? Why can't you do it? What could you do instead?

3 SPEAKING

A PAIR WORK Discuss the questions.

- What are young people allowed to do now that you weren't allowed to do when you were younger? Are you happy about this change?
- What are you required to do at work or school that you think you shouldn't have to do? Why?

> Young people are generally allowed to stay out later than I was. I don't think it's a good change because it can be dangerous to be out late at night.

> At school, we're required to sign the attendance list at the beginning of each class. I think we should choose which classes we want to attend.

4 FUNCTIONAL LANGUAGE

A Complete the conversation with the words and phrases below.

> apparently   going to believe   It wouldn't hurt
> kidding   you tried   wouldn't

A You're not ¹_____ what Pedro did last night. He arrived over an hour late to Gina's dinner party. And he didn't even apologize.

B No way! Are you ²_____ ?

A ³_____ , he thinks it's OK because no one said anything about it last night, but I think I'm going to say something to him today.

B I ⁴_____ do that if I were you.

A Why not? Don't you think it was rude?

B Sure. But it was Gina's party. It's really her place to talk to him if she was upset about it. Have ⁵_____ talking to her about it?

A No, but you know how she is, she wouldn't say anything even if she was upset.

B Maybe, but people generally don't like it when other people speak for them without their permission. ⁶_____ to at least talk to her about it first.

5 SPEAKING

A [PAIR WORK] **Choose one of the situations below. Act it out in pairs.**

1 Think of a difficult conversation you've had with a friend, a relative, or a coworker. Give details of what you said, and how the other person reacted.

    A A while ago I had a very tough conversation with a close friend who was always borrowing money but never paid me back.

    B Oh really? And what did you say to your friend?

2 You have been through a stressful personal experience. You want to convince your boss to let you take some time off. Get advice from your partner.

    A I'm so stressed out. I really need to take some time off, but we're so busy at the office right now.

    B Have you tried talking to your boss? You might want to …

B **Change roles and repeat the role play.**

UNIT OBJECTIVES

- speculate about events in the past
- talk about alternatives and possibilities
- keep your listener engaged
- write comments about things you can and can't live without
- share the story of an influential discovery or invention

START SPEAKING

A **What picture did these people want to take? How do you think the people feel about this photo? How would you feel?**

B **This is an example of "photobombing." Have you ever photobombed someone's picture, or has someone photobombed yours? Was it an accident or a joke?**

C **Have you ever taken a picture of something that went wrong in a funny or interesting way? For ideas, watch Andres's video.**

REAL STUDENT

Did something similar happen to you?

ACCIDENTAL DISCOVERIES

LESSON OBJECTIVE
■ speculate about events in the past

1 LANGUAGE IN CONTEXT

A   **Look at the pictures in the article. How are these two things connected? Read the article and check your answers.**

TOP 10 ACCIDENTAL DISCOVERIES

Author Mark Twain said, "*Accident* is the name of the greatest of all inventions."
Scientists carry out all kinds of **research** and face many **challenges** to make great **discoveries** and **breakthroughs**, but sometimes it is pure chance that provides the **solution**.

1 The Microwave Oven

In 1940, engineer Percy Lebaron Spencer was walking past an active magnetron in his lab when he noticed that the candy bar in his pocket had melted. Spencer was not the first to notice this **phenomenon**, but he decided to investigate it. If the candy hadn't melted, he wouldn't have made the **connection**, and we wouldn't have the microwave oven!

2 The Terracotta Army

The famous Terracotta Army was buried in Xian, China, about 2300 years ago. It was discovered by chance in 1974. If farmers hadn't needed to dig a well for water, they wouldn't have found the army. By studying the army, we have gained **knowledge** about ancient Chinese society. It has provided enormous **insight** into how Chinese emperors lived.

Read on to learn about #3 on the list →

FIND IT

B   PAIR WORK   **Which discovery do you think is more important? Why? What other accidental discoveries do you think are on the top 10 list? Use your phone to find other possibilities.**

2 VOCABULARY: Talking about discoveries

A   🔊 2.29   **Match the collocations to the correct definitions. Read the article again to help you. Then listen and check.**

1 find out something important	*a*	a make a discovery
2 prepare to do something that is new and difficult	___	b make a breakthrough
3 find out something important after working a long time	___	c face a challenge
4 get more information or understanding about something	___	d make a connection
5 study something formally	___	e provide insight
6 give the answer to a problem	___	f gain knowledge
7 join things together	___	g notice a phenomenon
8 give new understanding about something	___	h carry out research
9 see something that is happening and understand that it is important	___	i provide a solution

B   ▶ **Now go to page 150. Do the vocabulary exercises for 10.1.**

C   PAIR WORK   **Write sentences about issues that affect society today using the vocabulary and collocations above. Discuss the sentences with your classmates.**

> They have made breakthroughs in AIDS research, but they haven't found a cure yet.

3 GRAMMAR: Past unreal conditionals

A **Read the sentences in the grammar box, and then choose the correct option to complete the rules.**

> **Past unreal conditionals**
>
> If the candy **hadn't melted**, he **wouldn't have made** the connection.
> If farmers **hadn't needed** to dig a well, they **wouldn't have found** the army.

1 The sentences are about events from **the present / the past**.
2 The sentences are about actions that **really happened / didn't happen**.
3 The verb form in the *if* clause is **simple past / past perfect**. The main clause uses *would* (*not*) + *have* + **simple past / past participle**.

B ⯈ **Now go to page 138. Look at the grammar chart and do the grammar exercise for 10.1.**

C PAIR WORK **Complete the statements with the correct form of the verb in parentheses ( ).**
Do you know who or what the sentences refer to? (Answers at the bottom of the page.)

1 If he _____ (not sit) under an apple tree, he _____ (not discover) gravity.

2 If Frank Epperson _____ (not leave) his soda outside one cold night, the wooden stirring stick _____ (not freeze) in the cup, and we might not have these sweet summer treats today.

3 If Alexander Fleming _____ (not add) bacteria to the petri dish, he _____ (not invent) this life-saving drug.

4 If George Crum _____ (not slice) his potatoes extra thin, he _____ (not create) this popular snack.

5 Sylvan Goldman _____ (never think of) this helpful grocery store item if his office chair _____ (not be) on wheels.

4 SPEAKING

A PAIR WORK **Think about three things that you did earlier this week. Tell your partner and together imagine what would have happened if you hadn't done those things.**

> I left my house late, and I hit a terrible traffic jam on the way to class. If I'd left my apartment an hour earlier, I wouldn't have hit that traffic jam.

B GROUP WORK **Do the same thing in groups. Add to the chain of events to create stories. How long can you keep a logical chain of events going?**

> If my friend hadn't moved to Berlin, I might not have gone to Germany for vacation. I probably would have gone to Australia instead.

> If you had gone to Australia, what cities would you have visited?

BIG MISTAKE!

1 LANGUAGE IN CONTEXT

A 🔊 **2.30** **Look at the pictures on this page. What do you think happened in each one? Listen to the podcast and check your answers.**

🔊 **2.30 Audio script**

People **get things wrong** all the time, but some **mistakes** are bigger than others. At the 2016 Oscars ceremony, *La La Land* was wrongly declared Best Picture. The acceptance speeches had already begun when the **error** was discovered. The host had to **make it right** quickly. He apologized for the **mix-up** and announced the real winner, *Moonlight*.

Who was to **blame**? Some said the presenters should have checked the envelopes more carefully, but could it have been a simple **misunderstanding**? In the end, they discovered it was the **fault** of a backstage worker who gave the presenters the wrong envelope. He was tweeting! If he had paid attention, he could have **fixed the problem** in time, and the **confusion** never would have happened!

Other **blunders** live forever. In a 1986 World Cup match between England and Argentina, Diego Maradona scored the winning goal – with his hand! The referee should not have allowed the goal. If he had **corrected his mistake**, England might have won the World Cup. This **epic fail** became known as "the hand of God" goal!

2 VOCABULARY: Discussing right and wrong

A 🔊 **2.31** | PAIR WORK | **Look at the bold words in the script. Make a chart like the one below and write them into the correct category. Listen and check.**

Right / good behavior	Wrong / bad behavior
make something right	get something wrong

B ▶ **Now go to page 150. Do the vocabulary exercises for 10.2.**

C | PAIR WORK | **When was the last time you or someone you know made a big mistake? What was the mistake? Was it big enough to be called an epic fail? For ideas, watch Nicolle's video.**

REAL STUDENT

Was your mistake as bad as Nicolle's? Was it worse?

3 GRAMMAR: Modals of past probability

A **Read the sentences in the grammar box. Then choose the correct option to complete the rules.**

> **Modals of past probability**
>
> He **could have fixed** the problem.
> The referee **should not have allowed** the goal.
> England **might have won** the World Cup.

1 Use *could* and *might* to **criticize / suggest alternatives to** events from the past.
2 Use *should* to **criticize / suggest alternatives to** events from the past.
3 After the modal, use *have* + **past tense / past participle**.

B ▶ **Now go to page 139. Look at the grammar chart and do the grammar exercise for 10.2.**

C PAIR WORK **Have you ever regretted something you've said or done?**
1 Who was involved (a family member, a friend, a coworker, a stranger)?
2 What did you do or not do?
3 What could or should you have done differently?
4 Does your partner agree about what you could or should have done?

> I shouldn't have posted this one photo of my friend on social media. If I had asked her permission first, she might have said yes. But I didn't, and now she's mad at me.

4 SPEAKING

FIND IT

A GROUP WORK **Look at the pictures. What should the people have done differently? Share ideas about what might have happened and check your accuracy. You can find other pictures on your phone or online to speculate about.**

> In A, they shouldn't have put the plate of cookies so close to the edge of the table.

 ACCURACY CHECK

> When talking about the past, the modal verb *can* always changes to *could* in the affirmative.
>
> She ~~can~~ have gone to the store. ✗
> She could have gone to the store. ✓

> That might not have helped. The dog could have just jumped on the table.

1 FUNCTIONAL LANGUAGE

A 🔊 **2.32** **Look at the pictures. What mistake might a customer make about these two places? Listen to part of a conversation to check your answer.**

🔊 **2.32 Audio script**

A **… But that's not all!** We finally got to the hotel about midnight. We went to the check-in desk, but the clerk didn't have our reservation. **Wouldn't you know it?** I had booked the wrong hotel!

B Oh, no! How did you manage that?

A **You won't believe this, but** there are two hotels called The Miramar in that town – one in the city center, which I thought I had booked, and one about 20 kilometers away.

B So, what happened then?

A Well, **you can imagine.** We had to call another taxi, put all the bags back into the other car, and go to the other hotel. But **you know what?** It turned out the location was beautiful. That hotel was simpler than the one downtown, but the staff was really friendly, and, **are you ready for this?**

B What?

A They upgraded us to a bigger room! **Isn't that amazing?** I guess they felt sorry for us. Anyway, it was all so nice, we decided to go there again next summer!

B **Complete the chart with the bold expressions from the conversation.**

Keeping your listener engaged

But that's not ¹_____ !

² _____ you know it?

You won't ³_____ this, but …

You can ⁴_____ !

You ⁵_____ what?

Are you ⁶_____ for this?

Isn't that ⁷_____ ?

INSIDER ENGLISH

In conversation, *anyway* is commonly used as a way to change the subject, return to an earlier subject, or get to the most interesting point.

C 🔊 **2.33** **Complete the conversation with expressions from the chart. Listen and check.**

A OK, ¹_____ ? I had a job interview last week, for a web designer job, but the questions they asked me were all about sales.

B Sales? Why were they asking you about sales?

A Well, after like 20 minutes, I was wondering that myself, so I asked them. And, ² _____ ? I was in the wrong interview.

B No! That's so funny! You must have been so embarrassed!

A Oh, totally! But they were embarrassed, too. But ³_____ . I got it. I got the job! ⁴_____ ? I got the *wrong* job!

2 REAL WORLD STRATEGY

A 🔊 **2.34** Listen to two short conversations. What's the situation in each story?

> **SHOWING INTEREST IN A STORY**
>
> You can show interest in what someone is saying by interjecting some of these expressions:
>
> *Don't tell me you … !*
> *Let me guess – you … !*
> *That's (so) funny / strange / great / crazy / awful / sweet!*
> *You must be joking. / You can't be serious.*

B 🔊 **2.34** Read the information about showing interest in a story, and then listen again. How does the listener express interest in each story?

C ⬜ PAIR WORK Do a role play. Student A: Think of a common mistake that someone might make and create a story about it. Student B: Show that you are interested in the story. Switch roles and do it again.

3 PRONUNCIATION FOCUS: Saying long and short vowel sounds

A 🔊 **2.35** Listen and repeat. Focus on the **bold** vowel sounds.

Short vowel sounds	**a**dd	b**e**d	d**i**m	s**o**ck	c**u**b
Long vowel sounds	**ai**d	b**ea**d	d**i**me	s**oa**k	c**u**be

B 🔊 **2.36** Listen and repeat. Focus on the **bold** letters. Write L for a long vowel sound or S for a short vowel sound.

1 ho tel ___

2 ki lom et er ___

3 de ci ded ___

4 res er va tion ___

5 bags ___

6 a ma zing ___

C Look at the words in exercise B again. When a syllable ends in a vowel sound, is that vowel sound usually long or short?

4 SPEAKING

A Think of a true story from your life or a friend's life that people might find difficult to believe. Use the topics in the box to help you.

> family   health   sports   money   vacations   work

B ⬜ PAIR WORK Tell the story to your partner. Show interest and/or surprise when you listen to your partner's story.

> I found a wallet in the street with $100 in it. I turned it into the police.

> That's so nice! I think I might have kept it.

> Well, you won't believe this, but the owner gave me a reward – $100!

I CAN'T LIVE WITHOUT IT!

1 LISTENING

A **PAIR WORK** Look at the pictures. Which do you think gives a more realistic view of cars and driving today? Why?

B ◀) **2.37** **LISTEN FOR DETAILS** Listen to part of a podcast about the car and other inventions. Answer the questions.

1 What three bad inventions are mentioned at the beginning?
2 What does Renato compare the car to? According to him, what is the difference?
3 What does Paula like about cars?
4 What other three inventions are mentioned?
5 Which one do they finally agree about?

C ◀) **2.38** **PAIR WORK** **LISTEN FOR TONE** Read and listen to the extracts. Circle the tone that correctly describes the speaker's attitude.

1 It's part of my life.	positive	negative
2 Life would be better without them.	positive	negative
3 No one needs a machine for that.	aggressive	defensive
4 Are you sure about that?	aggressive	defensive

D **THINK CRITICALLY** Who do you agree with more, Renato or Paula? Of the four inventions discussed, which do you consider the best and worst? Why?

2 PRONUNCIATION: Listening for weak words

A ◀) **2.39** Listen to extracts from the podcast. Focus on the **bold** words. How is the sound different from the written words?

1 … could anyone have imagined how much we **would** depend on them one day?
2 Just think for a moment what life **would** be like without them.

B Choose the correct option to complete the statement.

Would is often weak when the word before it ends in a *consonant / vowel* sound.

3 **WRITING**

A Read the comment that was left on the podcast's website that expresses opinions about other inventions. How does the writer say we should judge whether an invention is good or bad?

INVENTIONS ☼ PODCAST   ⓐ Sign up   ⓢ Log in

COMMENTS

I enjoyed yesterday's show about the best and worst inventions. Both your guests had interesting points, but I think I agree more with Renato. He seemed more interested in an invention's impact on the planet and on society, whereas Paula seemed more interested in whether an invention made her life easier.

Personally, I think the worst inventions are the ones that harm the planet or society, even if they also happen to be really convenient. Cars definitely fit that category. Similarly, I would say that Styrofoam is a terrible invention.

Good inventions, by contrast, are ones that improve society or help the planet even if they create a little more work for us. Subways and other forms of public transportation are good examples. Sure, they might not always be as convenient as driving your own car, but they're way better for the environment.

🔍 5   ♡ 20   ⟳ 9

B **WRITING SKILL** Look again at the comment. Find the words that are used to show similarity and <u>underline</u> them. Find the words that are used to show contrast and (circle) them.

C **PAIR WORK** What inventions or discoveries could you not live without? Which ones do you wish didn't exist? What makes an invention good or bad in your view?

🧭 **WRITE IT**

D Write a comment similar to the one above expressing your opinion. Write about two things you couldn't live without and two things that you wish didn't exist. Use the phrases for similarities and contrasts from exercise B.

E **GROUP WORK** Share your comment with your classmates. How many people agree with you? How many disagree?

10.5 TIME TO SPEAK
TURNING POINTS

LESSON OBJECTIVE
- share the story of an influential discovery or invention

A   **DISCUSS**   In a group, look at the pictures. What early inventions or discoveries do they show? Which was invented or discovered first? Which was last? Put them in order.

FIND IT

B   Think about the modern discoveries and inventions below. How did each change human history? Think of two more big discoveries or inventions. You can use your phone to help you.

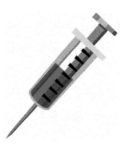 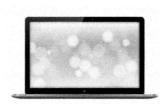 

C   **DECIDE**   Choose the invention or discovery that you agree has had the greatest impact on human history. Is it still important today? What would life be like without it (or if it had never been discovered or invented)? Think of at least five differences, both positive and negative.

D   **PRESENT**   Share your ideas with the class. One of you summarizes your discovery or invention, and the others each describe one way it changed human history.

E   **AGREE**   As a class, discuss the ideas presented. Which invention or discovery do you all think has had the greatest effect on human history? Is that effect mostly positive or mostly negative? Why do you think so?

To check your progress, go to page 156.

USEFUL PHRASES

DISCUSS
The invention of … was a turning point because …

…. changed history by …

DECIDE
I think the most important invention was …

If … hadn't been discovered, we wouldn't …

AGREE
I think group A's invention was the most important because…

… was a more important discovery than … because

UNIT OBJECTIVES

- discuss college life
- discuss scientific facts
- discuss alternatives and give recommendations
- write a comment presenting an argument
- present a proposal to solve a problem

CONTRASTS

11

START SPEAKING

A   Look at the picture. Where do you think the two men are? What's the difference between them?

B   Where and when do you wear formal clothes? Does the way you dress ever affect the way you feel or act?

C   Do you think it's true that people judge others by their appearance? Is that fair? Why or why not? For ideas, watch Nicolle's video.

REAL STUDENT

Do you agree with Nicolle?

11.1 STUDENT STORIES

1 LANGUAGE IN CONTEXT

A **What aspects of student life are shown in the brochure? Which are more academic and which are more social? Read about two students' experiences. Which aspects do they enjoy most?**

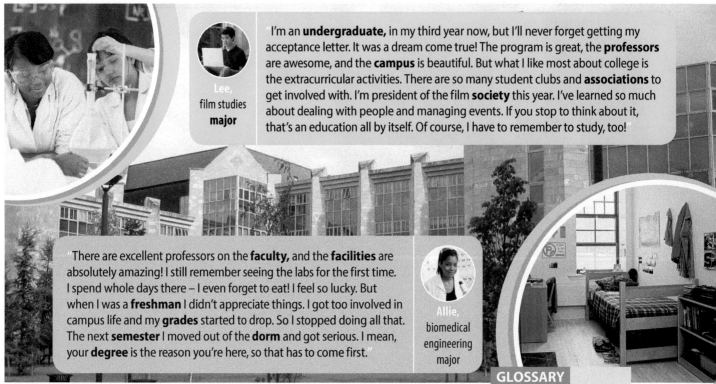

"I'm an **undergraduate,** in my third year now, but I'll never forget getting my acceptance letter. It was a dream come true! The program is great, the **professors** are awesome, and the **campus** is beautiful. But what I like most about college is the extracurricular activities. There are so many student clubs and **associations** to get involved with. I'm president of the film **society** this year. I've learned so much about dealing with people and managing events. If you stop to think about it, that's an education all by itself. Of course, I have to remember to study, too!"

Lee, film studies **major**

"There are excellent professors on the **faculty,** and the **facilities** are absolutely amazing! I still remember seeing the labs for the first time. I spend whole days there – I even forget to eat! I feel so lucky. But when I was a **freshman** I didn't appreciate things. I got too involved in campus life and my **grades** started to drop. So I stopped doing all that. The next **semester** I moved out of the **dorm** and got serious. I mean, your **degree** is the reason you're here, so that has to come first."

Allie, biomedical engineering major

GLOSSARY
extracurricular (*adj*) not part of academic study

2 VOCABULARY: Talking about college education

A 🔊 2.40 **Look at the bold words in the text. Write them in the correct categories. Then listen and check.**

People: _____ , _____ , _____ , _____

Places and buildings: _____ , _____ , _____

Academic life: _____ , _____ , _____ , _____

Organizations: _____ , _____

B ▶ **Now go to page 151. Do the vocabulary exercises for 11.1.**

C **PAIR WORK** **Discuss the questions.**

1 What is (or would be) the best and worst thing about being a freshman? Is it better to live in a dorm or an apartment as a freshman? As a sophomore, junior, or senior? Why?

2 What's the coolest major you can think of (oceanography, nuclear physics, musical theater, etc.)? Why do you think it's cool? Is it something you'd like to study?

! Generally speaking, undergraduates earn a bachelor's degree in four years: freshman (1st year), sophomore (2nd year), junior (3rd year), senior (last year(s)). These terms are nouns (people) or adjectives.

He's a sophomore now, but he's going to study in Spain his junior year.

Postgraduates earn a master's degree then a doctorate. There are no divisions by year.

He's getting his master's in economics.

3 GRAMMAR: Gerund and infinitive after *forget, remember, stop*

A Choose the correct answer to complete the rules. Use the sentences in the grammar box to help you.

1 When *forget, remember,* and *stop* are followed by a gerund (*-ing*),…

    a a definite action is finished.   **b** an action is general and indefinite.

2 When *forget, remember,* and *stop* are followed by an infinitive (*to* + verb),…

    a a definite action is finished.   **b** an action is general and indefinite.

> **Gerund and infinitive after *forget, remember, stop***
>
> I'll never **forget** <u>getting</u> my acceptance letter.   Sometimes I even **forget** <u>to eat</u>!
>
> I **remember** <u>seeing</u> them for the first time.   I have to **remember** <u>to study</u>, too!
>
> I **stopped** <u>doing</u> all that.   If you **stop** <u>to think</u> about it, that's an education all by itself.

B   PAIR WORK   **Discuss the differences in meaning in the sentence pairs. Say each sentence another way to make sure the meaning is clear.**

1 **a** I'll never forget meeting with my advisor for the first time.

    b I can't forget to meet with my advisor tomorrow!

2 **a** I remember putting my keys in my bag, but now I can't find them.

    b I have to remember to put the key in the mailbox before I leave.

3 **a** I stopped buying groceries at that store. It's so dirty.

    b I stopped to buy groceries on the way home.

C   ▶ **Now go to page 139. Do the grammar exercise for 11.1.**

D   GROUP WORK   **Complete these sentences so that they are true for you. Read your sentences to the group. Are any of your answers the same?**

1 After I get home tonight, I have to remember to …

2 Tomorrow, I can't forget to … or I'll be in trouble!

3 In the new year, I promise I'm going to stop …

4 SPEAKING

A **Choose one of the topics from the box. Think about the things you remember or something you'll never forget. For ideas, watch Tayra's video.**

> first day at school/on campus
> last day at school/on campus
> taking up a new sport or hobby
> giving up a sport or hobby

REAL STUDENT

Is your answer similar to Tayra's?

B   PAIR WORK   **Tell your partner about the topic you chose. Ask your partner questions about their experience to add details.**

C   GROUP WORK   **Tell your partner's story to other students.**

FOLK REMEDIES

1 LANGUAGE IN CONTEXT

A 🔊 **2.41** **A folk remedy is a medical treatment from long ago. Look at the pictures. What folk remedies might be connected to these foods? Listen to part of a podcast discussing folk remedies. Were you right?**

🔊 **2.41 Audio script**

Host	So, Dr. Wendt, are folk remedies usually based on **scientific** fact or are they just snake oil? For example, do carrots really help you see better at night?
Dr. Wendt	Not all folk remedies are backed up by real **science**, but that one is. Our **research** shows that the vitamin A in carrots can sharpen night vision. It's been **scientifically proven**.
Host	Great. So, is it also true that honey calms a cough and lets you sleep at night? I'd say yes to that one. I swear by it!
Dr. Wendt	You're right! It's true. **Medical researchers** have tested this, and there is **proof** that honey can be as effective as most cough **medicines**.
Host	So, my tea with honey is **medically approved**! That's good to know. OK, here's one from a listener: Does eating cheese before bed cause nightmares?
Dr. Wendt	I'm afraid there is no scientific **basis** to support the idea that cheese makes people have bad dreams. But a heavy meal, with or without cheese, may disturb your sleep or make you remember your dreams more clearly.

B 🔊 **2.41** **Listen again and read. What does science say about each of the folk remedies?**

INSIDER ENGLISH

We use the term *snake oil* to dismissively refer to something that does not give the positive results that it promises. The term originally referred to fake medicines, but it's now used for any product that does not deliver the benefits it claims.

2 VOCABULARY: Talking about science

A 🔊 **2.42** **Look at the bold words in the audio script and complete the chart. One word can be used twice. Listen and check.**

abstract noun	verb	person	adjective	compound adjective
_____		scientist	_____	_____
_____	research	_____		research-based
_____	prove		proven	_____
base/_____	base		based (on facts)	science-based
_____			medical	_____

B ▶ **Now go to page 151. Do the vocabulary exercises for 11.2.**

FIND IT

C Read some questions sent in by listeners of the full podcast. Do you know the answers? How could researchers test these ideas? If you can, use your phone to do some real research!

1 You said that people with red hair feel more pain. Is that a medical fact or an assumption based on reports from red-headed people?

2 Has research proven that it is better to wear dark-colored clothes in very hot, sunny places? It seems like light colors would be better.

3 I've read that some people (like taxi drivers, for example) are naturally better at navigation. Is there any scientific basis for that claim?

3 GRAMMAR: Causative verbs *help, let, make*

A Choose the correct option to complete the rules. Use the sentences in the grammar box to help you.

1 The verbs *help*, *let*, and *make* are used to talk about the effect caused by **something or someone else** / **our own actions**.

2 Causitive verbs are always used with another verb in the *to* + **verb** / **verb without** *to* form.

3 The object (*me, you, him, people*, etc.) goes **between** / **after** the two verbs.

> **Causative verbs *help, let, make***
>
> Carrots **help you see** better at night.
> Honey calms a cough and **lets you sleep** at night.
> Cheese **doesn't make people have** nightmares.

B ▶ **Now go to page 139. Do the grammar exercise for 11.2.**

C PAIR WORK Use the words to form questions. Check your accuracy. Then discuss the questions with your partner. Think of at least three answers for each one.

1 What / study / stay awake / you / can help / for a test ?

_____

2 sometimes / sleep / not let / What problems / you ?

_____

3 feel / makes / you / more relaxed / What / if stressed ?

_____

ACCURACY CHECK

Use the base form of the verb, NOT the *to* + verb form, after *help*, *let*, and *make*.

Carrots help you ~~to see~~ better at night. ✗

Carrots help you see better at night. ✓

4 SPEAKING

A GROUP WORK **Read the statements. Do people in your culture have the same beliefs? Which do you think might be based on real science? Why?**

■ Eating bread crusts will make your hair curl.

■ Eating oily fish helps you study better.

■ If you go outside with wet hair, you'll catch a cold.

■ Counting sheep helps you fall asleep.

■ A full moon makes people go a little crazy.

FIND IT

B What other folk remedies or beliefs do you know about? Do you think they might be based on science? You can use your phone to find out more.

11.3 CAN YOU SUGGEST AN ALTERNATIVE?

1 FUNCTIONAL LANGUAGE

A Look at the pictures of different kinds of mosquito repellent. Which ones have you tried? Can you think of others? Which ones do you think are the most effective? Why?

B ◀)) **2.43** Listen to a conversation between a pharmacist and a customer. Which repellent does the pharmacist recommend? What does the customer choose?

◀)) 2.43 Audio script

A Hi, I'm looking for a good mosquito repellent.

B Ah, yes. This one is scientifically proven to last at least eight hours. And this one's always worked well for me.

A Maybe not a spray. I don't think they're very healthy. **Can you suggest an alternative?** Do you have anything more natural?

B Well, **another option would be** these patches. They're 100% natural. Here, smell this. Can you smell the citronella?

A Yes. **That looks like a good alternative.** Do you put the patches on your skin?

B No, you put them on your clothes, or, for example, on the bed at night.

A No, **I'm looking for something different.** I mean, something you can actually wear.

B Well, we have these wristbands. **They're a good alternative.** They're 100% natural and should be effective for up to 12 hours. But **I don't think they're a great choice** for nighttime. I mean, you shouldn't wear them while you sleep.

A I see, so I could wear the wristband during the day and maybe use the patches at night. **That could work.**

B Yes, that's probably your best option.

C Complete the chart with the **bold** expressions from the conversation.

Asking for options	Suggesting alternatives
Do you have anything else?	You could also try …
1 _____ ?	3 _____ (these patches).
2 _____ .	4 _____ .

Discussing disadvantages	Responding to suggestions
It might not be the best option.	I like that option.
5 _____ (for nighttime).	6 _____ .
	7 _____ .

D [PAIR WORK] Discuss the possible alternatives in these situations. Use the expressions in the chart.

1 You want to go out for dinner, but you don't want to spend too much money.

2 You want to take up a new sport, but you don't have much free time.

> We could try the food court at the mall. There's a good salad bar there.

> But it's so crowded there. I don't think …

2 REAL WORLD STRATEGY

GIVING A PERSONAL RECOMMENDATION
Use these expressions when you want to give a personal recommendation.
This one's always worked well for me.
If I were you, I'd choose/pick/go with …
I've always had luck with …

A   🔊 **2.44**   PAIR WORK   Read the information in the box about giving a personal recommendation. Then listen to two short conversations. What are they talking about? Which expressions from the box do they use?

1 Topic: _____

Expression: _____

2 Topic: _____

Expression: _____

B   PAIR WORK   Think of a time when you gave a personal recommendation to someone. What was it for? What was your recommendation? What were your reasons for it?

REGISTER CHECK

When giving advice, avoid using imperative statements. Use "I statements" to show that you respect the other person's perspective and don't want to force your opinion on them.

~~Buy this one. It's the best.~~
I've always had good luck with this one.

3 PRONUNCIATION FOCUS: Stressing long words

A   🔊 **2.45**   Listen and repeat. How many syllables are in each word?

1 scientifically _____   4 situation _____
2 alternatives _____   5 recommendation _____
3 disadvantages _____

B   🔊 **2.45**   Listen again. Which syllable is stressed? ⟨Circle⟩ it.

C   PAIR WORK   Practice saying the words in exercise 3A with a partner. Does your partner stress the correct syllable?

4 SPEAKING

A   **Look at the pictures of laptop bags and prepare to perform a role play. Prepare for both roles by yourself (not with a partner).**

Customer: You want to buy a bag for your laptop. You're not sure which to buy. Think about your needs and your style. Prepare some questions for the sales clerk.

Sales clerk: Think of some good points about each of the bags. Think about which bag you would recommend to different people in different situations or with different needs.

B   PAIR WORK   Do the role play two times, once as the customer and once as the sales clerk. Then do a new role play using your story from exercise 2B or a new idea. You can be in a store or talking with a coworker or friend.

DRIVERLESS CARS? NO WAY!

LESSON OBJECTIVE
- write a comment presenting an argument

1 READING

A **Look at the picture. Do you think it shows a positive view of technology? Why or why not?**

B **INFERRING ATTITUDE** **Read the opinion piece on the role of technology in our lives. Which sentence best describes the writer's attitude?**

a Technology is ruining our lives, so we should reject it in favor of real experiences.

b Technology will reduce our ability to experience life's pleasures if we're not careful.

c Technological developments are good only if they make life easier.

Embrace the technical revolution? **Not me!**

Dishwashers, cell phones, the internet – all great inventions that make life easier, more comfortable, and more fun. But when technology goes too far, it automates experiences and takes the enjoyment out of life.

Take driverless cars. Or in my case, don't take them! I love driving my car. I love to feel the wheels respond to my touch. I love to drive long hours on empty roads, with my hand hanging out the window, feeling the wind between my fingers. I don't want the car to drive me, and half the American population are with me on this.

Another example of unwanted technology takeover is robot waiters. Do you really want your meal served by a machine? I can see it might appeal to children, but where's the human touch – the shared smile, the pleasant banter, the thoughtful attention? Robot waiters are becoming more and more popular in Asia, and the trend is surely going to spread.

In the world of entertainment, people once worried that live streaming would kill live events. Statistics show, however, that more and more people are attending live concerts and music festivals all around the world. The urge to share an experience, to feel the buzz of thousands of other people, is stronger than the lazy comforts of technological shortcuts.

Technology can, no doubt, make life a lot easier in many ways, but we need to make sure it isn't robbing us of the real pleasures that make life worth living.

GLOSSARY
embrace (v) accept with enthusiasm
automate (v) use machines to do something
banter (n) light, funny conversation
buzz (n) excitement

C **IDENTIFYING ARGUMENTS** **Read the opinion piece again. What are the writer's arguments against the following examples of technology?**

Driverless cars

Robot waiters

Streaming live events

D **THINK CRITICALLY** **Do you agree with the writer? Why or why not? Do you think she may be exaggerating? Why or why not? What are some other examples of technology that's "gone too far" in your opinion? Why do you think so?**

2 WRITING

A Read a comment that was posted in response to the opinion piece. Does the writer generally agree or disagree with the original piece? Do you agree with the writer's arguments? Why or why not?

> ### Embrace the technical revolution? Yes, please!
>
> **First of all** I'd like to say that, as much as I love technology, I think there are times when we need to get back to basics. Live music is so much better when you're there in person, and I may be old-fashioned, but I much prefer a paperback to an e-reader. But those are just my preferences, and I totally respect the fact that others may not agree with me.
>
> **Where I strongly disagree with the article is** on the point of driverless cars. Research suggests that the use of driverless cars would help the flow of traffic, and **more importantly**, it could reduce the number of accidents significantly. **It's also important to remember that** driverless cars don't speed, they don't run red lights, and they aren't impatient. **Additionally,** they will help elderly people and the disabled travel independently. **And finally,** they're optional. If you really want to drive yourself, no one's going to stop you.

B **PAIR WORK** **WRITING SKILL** Look at the **bold** phrases in the text. Which are used for each purpose?

1 to begin an argument: _____

2 to add a new argument: _____

3 to conclude: _____

C **PAIR WORK** Think of three arguments for and three arguments against robot waiters. Which arguments do you think are the most convincing? Why?

 **WRITE IT**

D Follow the steps to write your own comment in response to the opinion piece.

1 Choose a title:

Robot waiters? Yes, please!   *Robot waiters? No way!*

2 Choose the three points (for <u>or</u> against) you want to include from exercise C.

3 Read the opinion piece and the comment above again. Choose the transition phrases that work best for your points.

4 Write your comment. Write about 150 words.

E **GROUP WORK** Read all the comments. Make a note of any particularly convincing arguments. Then vote on whether you think robot waiters are generally a positive or negative innovation. Share your ideas with the class.

TIME TO SPEAK
MEDIATION

A Look at the picture. Where do you think this tree is? What problems might the tree cause for the people who use this area?

B PREPARE The tree has grown too big, and the people in the building are going to hold a meeting to decide what to do about it. Divide into three groups to prepare for the meeting.

Group A: You like having a tree here, so you want to replace this tree with a smaller one. Think about arguments for having a tree near the building.

Group B: You think this area could be used for more useful purposes, like extra parking space. Think about arguments for other ways to use this space.

Group C: You are the mediators. You will listen to both sides and try to help them reach a compromise. Discuss possible arguments and suggestions you could make to keep both sides happy.

C DISCUSS Now make new groups of three, with one student from each group. Students from Group A and Group B put forward their arguments, and the Group C student mediates and tries to help the others come to an agreement.

D PRESENT The Group C students report back on the discussions to the class. Listen to all the solutions. Who has the best solution? Take a class vote to decide.

To check your progress, go to page 156.

USEFUL PHRASES

PREPARE
One argument for keeping/ removing the tree is …
Another good argument might be …
As an alternative, we could …

DISCUSS
We think it's really important to …
We need to consider …
Would you consider … ?

PRESENT
The main arguments for/ against keeping it were …
In the end, we decided to …
We couldn't come to an agreement because …

UNIT OBJECTIVES
- describe a special photo and the story behind it
- discuss childhood memories
- recall and share past experiences
- write a summary and response about keeping pets
- recall and discuss a national moment

LOOKING BACK

12

START SPEAKING

A   Look at the picture for 15 seconds, then cover it. Make a detailed list of things in the picture.

B   Compare your list with other classmates. How many things did they remember that you didn't? What things are in the picture but not on anyone's list? Why do you think some things were more memorable than others?

C   Do you have a good memory for names, dates, or faces? How easily do you remember facts, stories, or appointments? For ideas, watch Andres's video.

REAL STUDENT

How does your memory compare with Andres's?

PHOTO STORIES

1 LANGUAGE IN CONTEXT

A **Look at the pictures and read the stories about them. Match the people to the pictures. What does the picture represent for them?**

A

B

C

Gary, Trenton, New Jersey, U.S.A.

What I remember most about my childhood is my pet dog, Milo. Here, I'm 10 and in our back yard with him. I loved that **fresh** smell of grass. I can almost feel his **smooth** fur and **damp** breath now. (Sometimes it was pretty **stinky**, but I didn't care.) The thing I love about this photo is that it brings back all those **bright** summer days.

Sonia, San Miguel de Allende, Mexico

The air in my grandma's house was **scented** with spices. She baked all kinds of **flavorful** cakes decorated with **colorful** icing. The thing I liked most was licking the **tasty** icing off my fingers. She called me her "helper"! What I love about this photo is that it helps me remember our special relationship.

Alex, Kingston, Jamaica

What I miss most about my grandpa are the hours we spent listening to music. This picture represents that for me. I remember his record cabinet had a **musty** smell, but I liked it. His hands were big and **rough**, but he handled those records so gently. He'd sing along with a **deep, melodic** voice. My voice sounded so **high-pitched** next to his!

B PAIR WORK **Which of the senses – touch, smell, taste, sound, sight – do the people mention? What do they talk about exactly?**

Sonia talks about the smell of spices in the air.

2 VOCABULARY: Talking about the senses

A 🔊 2.46 **Look at the bold adjectives in the stories. Write which sense they describe. Listen and check. Which ones usually describe a positive sensation? A negative sensation? Neither?**

Smell: _____ , _____ , _____ , _____

Sound: _____ , _____ , _____

Touch: _____ , _____ , _____

Taste: _____ , _____

Sight: _____ , _____

B ▶ **Now go to page 152. Do the vocabulary exercises for 12.1.**

C PAIR WORK **Describe some of the things that you have experienced today using sense adjectives.**

I opened the curtain and the light was really bright… I hate mornings!

3 GRAMMAR: Adding emphasis

A **Choose the correct option to complete the rules. Use the sentences in the grammar box to help you. Can you find two more examples in the text?**

1 To give emphasis and focus to an idea, you can use the phrase "*What I* + verb" OR "*The thing I* + verb" at the **end / beginning** of the sentence.

2 The thing you want to emphasize comes at the **end / beginning** of the sentence.

3 Use the verb *be* / *have* to link the two parts of the sentence together.

> **Adding emphasis**
>
> **What I remember** most about my childhood **is** my pet dog, Milo.
> **The thing I liked** most **was** licking the tasty icing off my fingers.

B ▶ **Now go to page 140. Look at the grammar chart and do the grammar exercise for 12.1.**

C PAIR WORK **Rewrite the sentences and add emphasis.**

1 I really liked the sunroof in my family's old car.

   The thing I really liked about my family's old car was the sunroof.

2 As a child I loved mangoes more than anything!

3 I miss cooking with my grandma most of all.

4 From my childhood I remember riding on trains most clearly.

5 As a teenager I really loved skateboarding.

D PAIR WORK **Are the sentences in exercise C true for you? If not, change them to make them true.**

> *I didn't like mangoes. The thing I loved as a child was ice cream!*

4 SPEAKING

FIND IT

A PAIR WORK **Find a photo on your phone or other device that you could post to an online forum. Describe the story behind it. Use sense adjectives to describe how you felt in the photo.**

> *I was at the beach on vacation. What I remember about that moment was the salty smell of the sea and the fresh wind in my face.*

B GROUP WORK **Share your photos and stories with the rest of the group. Which ones involve the most senses?**

DID THAT REALLY HAPPEN?

1 LANGUAGE IN CONTEXT

A ◀) **2.47** **The title of this podcast is "Did it really happen?" What do you think it's about? Listen and check your answer.**

◀) 2.47 Audio script

Has something ever **brought back** a **vivid** memory, but later you find out it never actually happened? Most people feel sure about the accuracy of their own memories of their own life. I know I do, but how trustworthy are our **early** memories really? Listen to David's story:

*"In 2nd grade, a new student, Nolan, arrived at my boarding school. We became friends, and he came home with me for winter break once because his family lived far away. I have a very **clear** memory of all this when I **look back on** it. Even today, the smell of burning wood **reminds me of** winter breaks spent sitting in front of the fire, especially the one with Nolan.*

*Forty years later I met Nolan again. He didn't **recognize** me at first or remember much about that time. He had a **vague** memory of me, but he was positive that he had never stayed with my family. I was shocked!"*

Our **long-term** memory can play tricks on us. Psychiatrist Rochelle Rivas explains:

*"The more often you **recall** a specific memory, the more distorted it becomes. It's like making a copy of a copy of a copy. That's why this only happens with **distant** or **childhood** memories, not with **short-term** or **recent** ones."*

Do you have a false memory? If so, send us an email and tell us about it.

B ◀) **2.47** **Listen again and read along. Choose the correct words to complete the sentences.**
1 Nolan and David *stayed friends / lost contact*.
2 Nolan and David recall their time together *the same way / differently*.
3 Dr. Rivas compares recalling distant memories to *recalling short-term ones / making copies of copies*.

C PAIR WORK **Do you have a memory that other people say happened differently? Is there any way to find out who's right? Do you think people sometimes distort memories on purpose? Why or why not?**

2 VOCABULARY: Describing memories

A ◀) **2.48** **Listen and say the words in the box. Categorize the words into adjectives and verbs. Which adjectives are opposites of each other? What verb is a synonym for all the verbs here?**

bring back	childhood	clear	distant
early	long-term	look back on	recall
recent	recognize	remind of	short-term
vague	vivid		

> **!** *remember* vs. *remind of*
> *"I **remember** you."* but *"You **remind me of** my cousin. You are similar in many ways."*

B ▷ **Now go to page 152. Do the vocabulary exercises for 12.2.**

3 GRAMMAR: Substitution and referencing

A **Choose the best option to complete the rules. Use the sentences in the grammar box to help you.**

1 To avoid repeating **an uncountable / a countable** noun, we can use *one / ones*.

2 To avoid repeating a verb or verb phrase, we can use the auxiliary verb for that tense. For example, in the present tense, we use *so / do*.

3 To avoid repeating a question, we can use *so / do*.

4 To reference a noun or noun phrase, we can use *it/them* for **specific things / whole ideas** and *this/that* for **specific things / whole ideas**.

Substitution

That reminds me of <u>winter breaks</u>, especially the **one** with Nolan.

Most people <u>feel sure about the accuracy of their memories</u>. I know I **do**.

<u>Do you have a false memory</u>? If **so**, send us an email.

Referencing

When you recall <u>a memory</u> often, **it** becomes distorted.

<u>When you recall a memory often, it becomes distorted</u>. That's why **this** only happens with distant memories.

B ▶ **Now go to page 140. Do the grammar exercise for 12.2.**

C PAIR WORK **Read the conversation. Change the <u>underlined</u> words to substitutions or referents. Then check your accuracy.**

A Do you have a favorite childhood memory? If ¹<u>you have a favorite childhood memory</u>, tell me about ²<u>your favorite childhood memory</u>.

B No, I ³<u>don't have a favorite childhood memory</u>. But did I tell you about the time I met Harrison Ford?

A No, you never told me about ⁴<u>the time you met Harrison Ford</u>! I love to hear celebrity-sighting stories.

B I know! I ⁵<u>love to hear celebrity-sighting stories</u>, too! And I really like telling ⁶<u>celebrity-sighting stories</u>.

> ✓ **ACCURACY** CHECK
>
> When substituting with *one/ones*, make sure the pronoun agrees with what it is substituting.
>
> *It happens with childhood memories, not recent ~~one~~.* ✗
> *It happens with childhood memories, not recent ones.* ✓

4 SPEAKING

A **Look at the pictures. Do you remember these things? If so, what kinds of childhood memories do they bring back for you?**

B PAIR WORK **Discuss the questions.**

1 What kinds of things do you look back on most fondly (with nice feelings) – school days, family events, sports events, etc.?

2 Think about a time when you met an old friend. Did you recognize each other? What did you talk about? Did you remember events from your past the same way or differently?

3 Think about a nice early memory. Is it possible that someone told you about it and that you don't really remember it at all?

1 FUNCTIONAL LANGUAGE

A 🔊 2.49 **Look at the picture of old friends sharing memories. Listen to their conversation. Why is Rebecca frustrated with Peter?**

🔊 2.49 Audio script

A That reminds me of the White Mountains. **Do you remember that time** we got lost there, Peter? It was getting really dark, and we didn't know which way to go. Remember? It was about five years ago …

B We got lost?

A **Don't tell me you don't remember.**

B I remember us hiking in the White Mountains, but **I don't recall getting lost.** But you know how my memory is. And **that whole period's a bit vague** anyway. I've kind of blocked things out around then.

A But it was, like, really scary.

B Yeah, I just don't … What happened exactly?

A We got lost! And then your flashlight didn't work, and I totally panicked …

B The flashlight – yeah, **that rings a bell.** Yeah, **it's all coming back to me now.** Just after that we found the path again, right?

A Right!

B And it turned out that we were, like, only a hundred meters from the campground!

B **Complete the chart with the bold expressions from the conversation.**

Prompting a response	Recalling a memory
Do you remember that ¹_____ we … ?	I don't ³_____ (getting lost).
Don't ²_____ me you don't remember.	That (whole period's) a bit ⁴_____ anyway!
	That ⁵_____ a bell!
	It's all ⁶_____ back to me now.

C 🔊 **2.50** **Complete the conversation with expressions from the chart. Listen and check.**

A ¹_____
that time you went to the airport without
your passport?

B Oh, come on. I never did that.

A Yes, you did! ²_____
_____ you don't remember! We had
to go back home and get it, and then we
spent a fortune on a new flight. You had to
ask Mom and Dad for a loan …

B Oh, OK. That ³_____
_____. We were going to Cancun,
right?

A Yes! And we had to wait, like, five hours for
the next flight.

B OK, yeah. It's ⁴_____
_____ to me now! I don't think I
ever paid Mom and Dad back for that. Don't
remind them!

2 REAL WORLD STRATEGY

A 🔊 **2.51** **Listen to a short conversation. What's the initial memory? What similar memories does the other person share?**

> **SHARING EXPERIENCES**
>
> When you want to share a similar story, or invite others to do so, use these phrases:
>
> *That reminds me of a story. …*   *That's like the time that …*
> *I had a similar experience once. …*   *Has that ever happened to you?*

B 🔊 **2.51** **Read about sharing experiences in the box above. Listen again. Which phrases do the people use?**

C PAIR WORK **Have a conversation in which you share a memory. Your partner then shares a similar or related experience from their own life.**

3 PRONUNCIATION FOCUS: Saying consonant clusters

A 🔊 **2.52** **Listen. Write the missing letters.**

1 _____ocked
2 hun_____eds
3 _____ashlight
4 camp_____ound
5 experie_____e
6 pani_____ed

B 🔊 **2.52** PAIR WORK **Listen again. Practice saying the words. Does your partner say each word clearly?**

4 SPEAKING

A PAIR WORK **Do a role play in which two friends recall a memory. Student A recalls the memory and gives details to help Student B remember it. Student B doesn't recall it at first but remembers more as details are given, and adds details, too.**

> Don't tell me you don't
> remember the time we … ?

> I don't quite recall that.
> What happened exactly?

> Come on. We were in Hawaii …

B GROUP WORK **Expand the role play with a third person in the conversation. Student C shares a similar experience from their own past. Change roles and add more details each time.**

MAN'S BEST FRIEND?

1 LISTENING

A **PAIR WORK** Look at the pictures. What are the dogs doing in each picture? What kinds of relationship do these animals have with people?

B 🔊 **2.53** Listen to a debate about people and their dogs. Who mentions the dogs in the pictures, Kenan or Lucia? What do they say about them? Are their opinions positive or negative?

C 🔊 **2.54** **PAIR WORK** **LISTEN FOR EXAMPLES** Both Kenan and Lucia use examples to support their arguments. Listen to the extracts and write the phrases you hear to introduce examples.

1 _____ For instance, ...
2 _____
3 _____
4 _____
5 _____
6 _____

D **PAIR WORK** **THINK CRITICALLY** Who do you think made a stronger case, the affirmative side (Kenan) or the opposition (Lucia)? Why? What was the strongest point in their argument?

We liked Lucia's argument, but her point about service dogs wasn't relevant. The topic is about pets.

E Think about your culture and its attitude towards dogs. What is their role in society? Do you agree with that role? Why or why not? For ideas, watch Alessandra's video.

REAL STUDENT

Do you agree with Alessandra?

2 PRONUNCIATION: Listening for transitions

A 🔊 **2.55** **Listen to the excerpts from the debate. Focus on the bold words.**

1 Team A argued that people shouldn't keep dogs as pets and Team B argued that they should. **To finish the debate**, we'll hear a summary of each group's position …

2 All those jobs help people and they keep the dogs happy and active. So, **in conclusion**, we'd actually be helping dogs a lot more by keeping them as working animals …

3 So, **to sum up**, there are many ways that dogs and humans help each other.

B **Choose the correct option to complete the statement.**

Speakers often say words with *more / less* stress and *higher / lower* intonation to mark and transition to a summary statement.

3 WRITING

A **Read one student's summary of Lucia's side of the debate and his own response to it. Does he basically agree or disagree with Lucia's argument?**

> Lucia argues that dogs should be kept as pets, and she supports that argument with three points. She says that dogs are more predictable and reliable than people. While this may be true, the company of a dog isn't the same as the company of a person. So despite the fact that dogs are trustworthy, it's not a good argument for why we should keep them as pets. She also says that keeping a dog as a pet is good for children because it teaches them to be caring and responsible; however, there are lots of other ways to teach children responsibility. Finally, she points out that dogs help society as service animals for blind people or as police dogs. Although that is true, those dogs aren't pets. They are working dogs.

B PAIR WORK WRITING SKILL **Identify and ⌢circle⌢ the words and phrases used to link contrasting ideas in the summary. Then use the phrases you circled to link the ideas below.**

1 Dogs are cute. They should not be kept as pets.

2 Most dogs are predictable and friendly. Some dogs are unpredictable and dangerous.

WRITE IT

C PAIR WORK **Write your own summary of and response to Kenan's opinion. In your response, be sure to …**
- mention points that you agree and disagree with.
- use appropriate language to contrast ideas.

D PAIR WORK **Read another pair's summary and response. Did you include the same information? Do you agree with their response? Why or why not?**

The other pair didn't mention how dogs help children. We think that is an important and original idea.

TIME TO SPEAK
Where were you when … ?

A Read the blog post about a memory. How does the writer describe the memory?
Why does she call it a "national moment"?

I had the strangest experience today. I was surfing YouTube and I ran across a clip of when Michael Phelps won his seventh gold medal for swimming in the 2008 Olympics. Wow, I remember that so well! It was one of those national moments, where everyone remembers exactly where they were when it happened. I was at my friend's house. What I remember most is how we were all literally yelling at the TV, cheering him on. And I remember being so excited because he won by a lot. But the thing is, I was watching the clip today, and it was actually a really close race. I mean he only won by like, 1/100th of a second!

FIND IT

B **PREPARE** Think of a "national moment" from your country's history during your lifetime. It could be something from sports, politics, entertainment, or something else. You can use your phone to help you.

C **DECIDE** In small groups, share the national moments you thought of. Choose one and discuss your memories of it.
- Where were you when it happened?
- What do you remember most about the event?
- Does everyone in the group remember it the same way, or are your memories of the event different? If so, how? Why do you think they are different?

D **PRESENT** Choose someone to present your group's national moment to the class. Describe it but don't say what it was, so the rest of the class has to guess. Does everyone in the class remember the event? Does anyone remember it differently?

To check your progress, go to page 156.

USEFUL PHRASES

PREPARE
What about when … ?
Do you remember when … ?
An event I really remember was when …

DECIDE
What I remember most about … was …
Really? The way I remember it was …

PRESENT
The things we remembered most about this event were …
Oh! I know. It was when …
But I remember it differently. The way I remember it, …

REVIEW 4 (UNITS 10–12)

1 VOCABULARY

A Put the words and phrases into the correct categories. There are five items for each category.

breakthrough	dorm	bring back	stinky	degree	bright	epic fail
phenomenon	fault	freshman	insight	knowledge	tasty	major
misunderstanding	recall	melodic	recognize	remind of	error	research
undergraduate	smooth	confusion	look back on			

1 Discoveries: _____

2 Mistakes: _____

3 College: _____

4 Senses: _____

5 Memory: _____

B Add two more words or phrases to each category.

2 GRAMMAR

A Complete the conversation with the correct form of the verbs in parentheses ( ).

A I shouldn't [1]_____ (buy) this new car. It was way too expensive. I really can't afford it.

B Did you stop [2]_____ (think) about that before you [3]_____ (buy) it? You could [4]_____ (wait) a year or two. Your old car was still in good condition.

A You're right. If I [5]_____ (not buy) the car, I [6]_____ (spend) all my savings. And I [7]_____ (not have to) borrow money from my parents.

B PAIR WORK   What have you done recently that you regret? Talk about it with your partner.

C Choose the correct words to complete the paragraph. Then change the underlined parts of the paragraph to make it true for you.

I'll never forget underline{our family vacations at the beach}. Those memories make me [1]*feel / to feel* underline{happy}. The thing I liked most underline{about those vacations} [2]*was / were* underline{building huge sand castles with my brother}. And I remember [3]*to spend / spending* underline{hours in the water with my father}. It was underline{so much fun}. Of course, there were some negative memories, too. But we all tend to remember only the positive [4]*one /ones*.

3 SPEAKING

A PAIR WORK   What have you done today? What would have happened if things had been different?

> Today I overslept, so I didn't have time for breakfast. I'm really hungry now. If I hadn't overslept, I'd have had breakfast, and I wouldn't be so hungry now.

B Tell the class what you learned about your partner.

4 FUNCTIONAL LANGUAGE

A **Use the words and phrases in the box to complete the conversation.**

a good alternative	won't believe	another option	could work	don't tell me
ever happened	I've always had luck	ready for this	that time	amazing

A You [1]_____ this, but I just washed my phone in the washing machine.

B [2]_____ you had left it in the pocket of your pants.

A Exactly. And are you [3]_____?

B What?

A The phone's still working. Isn't that [4]_____?

B That's incredible.

A I know, totally! Has that [5]_____ to you?

B Well, not in the washing machine, but do you remember [6]_____ when I dropped my phone in the swimming pool? It never worked again.

A You should buy a phone like this. [7]_____ with this brand.

B But it's pretty expensive.

A [8]_____ would be a waterproof case for the phone. That's [9]_____.

B That [10]_____. I guess I'll get myself one.

5 SPEAKING

A PAIR WORK **Choose one of the situations below. Act it out in pairs.**

1 You're looking for a waterproof case for your phone, or another gadget you need. Get recommendations and discuss alternatives.

   A I'm looking for a waterproof case for my phone.

   B This one is waterproof and it's good up to 30 feet deep in the water.

   A I don't need anything that extreme. Can you suggest an alternative?

2 Talk about an event or mistake that had unexpected consequences.

   A You'll never guess what happened to me this morning.

   B Don't tell me you took the wrong bus again.

   A Worse than that. I went all the way to my old job. And you know what? I met my old boss and she asked me to come back to the company!

3 You meet an old school friend and start talking about your days in middle school.

   A Do you remember that time you made me skip class and go to the mall with you?

   B I don't recall skipping classes in middle school.

   A Are you kidding me? Remember we bumped into your aunt and …

B **Change roles and repeat the role play.**

GRAMMAR REFERENCE AND PRACTICE

7.1 REPORTED STATEMENTS (PAGE 67)

> **Reported statements**
>
> To report and summarize what someone said, we use a past reporting verb. We often report the words in a past tense, too.
>
> "I **feel** much closer to my family." → He **explained** that he **felt** much closer to his family.
>
> "Their use **has multiplied** in recent years." → They **reported** that their use **had multiplied** in recent years.
>
> To report instructions we use a reporting verb + person + (*not*) *to* + verb. We can also use other types of verbs like *persuade* or *convince*.
>
> "Buy a cell phone!" → They **told / persuaded us to buy** a cell phone.

A **Change the sentences from direct speech to reported speech.**

1 "I prefer speaking face to face over texting or sending messages."

He said that _____

2 "Get a new computer!"

She told _____

3 "That's why you should buy a new smartphone, not a tablet."

He convinced _____

4 "We won first prize in the competition."

They explained _____

5 "I will text you when I leave work."

She said _____

7.2 REPORTED QUESTIONS (PAGE 69)

A **Change the questions from direct speech to reported speech.**

1 Why did you buy a new smartphone?

He asked _____

2 Do you prefer to speak on the phone or by text messages?

She asked _____

3 Will you get a new tablet for your birthday?

We asked her _____

4 Can you help me with this computer problem?

I asked them _____

5 How many friends did you meet on Facebook?

She asked him _____

8.1 PRESENT UNREAL CONDITIONALS (PAGE 77)

Present unreal conditionals		
Present unreal conditionals refer to imagined present or future situations. They have two parts:		
<u>The *if* clause</u> introduces or describes an **imagined situation**		<u>The main clause</u> asks about or discusses **an imagined reaction**
The verb is in the simple past, but it does NOT refer to a past time.		Use the modal verb *would* or *might* + verb for statements, questions, and short answers.
Statement	If I **didn't have** a family,	I'**d do** it.
	If I **was/were** single,	I **might do** it.
	Even if you **paid** me a million dollars	I **wouldn't do** it.
Question	If you **saw** this job ad,	**would** you **click** on the link?
Short answers	Yes, I **would / might**.	No, I **wouldn't**.

When the *if* clause comes first, it ends with a comma:

   If you wanted a new job, would you look online?

When the main clause comes first, no comma is necessary:

   Would you look online if you wanted a new job?

In the *if* clause, you can use either *was* or *were* with *I, he, she, it*:

   If he were/was single, he'd do it.

   If it were/was a full-time job, I'd take it.

   I'd accept the job if I was/were you.

A **Choose the correct words to complete the sentences.**

1 If *I had / I'd* more time, *I did / I'd take* piano lessons.

2 If *I lived / I'd live* in a smaller town, *I can / I'd be able* to get to work faster.

3 If my job *had paid / paid* better, *I felt / I'd feel* happier about it.

4 If *I could / I'd be able to* live anywhere in the world, *I chose / I'd choose* to live in the Rockies.

5 *Would / Had* you move to a new place for a job if you *didn't know / hadn't known* anyone there?

6 I don't think I *would agree / agreed* to live alone for a long time, even if the place *were / had been* beautiful.

8.2 *I WISH* (PAGE 79)

I wish
We use *I wish* to express a desire for something to be different, or feelings of sadness or regret.
Talking about the present: use the simple past.
I **don't have** any free time ➔ I wish I **had** more free time.
Talking about the future: use the simple past, the past continuous, or modal verbs *would* and *could*.
I **work** every weekend. ➔ I wish I **didn't work** every weekend.
I'**m working** this weekend ➔ I wish I **wasn't working** next weekend.
I **can't take** time off. ➔ I wish I **could take** time off.
Talking about the past: use the past perfect.
I **didn't study** for the exam. ➔ I wish I **had studied** for the exam.

A **Change the statements to wishes.**

I'm leaving tomorrow. → I wish I wasn't leaving tomorrow.

1 I can't speak Japanese. _____

2 I didn't finish my report last night. _____

3 I don't have any free time this weekend. _____

4 I can't go on vacation this summer. _____

5 I have an assignment to finish tonight. _____

6 I spent all my money on a new computer. _____

9.1 PROHIBITION, PERMISSION, OBLIGATION (PRESENT) (PAGE 87)

Prohibition, permission, obligation (present)	
We can use a range of expressions to talk about permission, prohibition, and obligation in the present.	
Prohibition	You **may not / aren't allowed to / aren't supposed to** wear a hoodie. note: *may not* and *be (not) required to* are stronger than *be (not) supposed to*
Permission	You **are allowed to / may** bring your guide dog inside.
Obligation	You **are supposed to / are required to** wear a seatbelt. note: *be required to* is stronger than *be supposed to*

A **Replace the bold words with expressions from the box. Use the negative form where necessary.**

be allowed to   be required to   be supposed to   can   may

1 You **can't** eat or drink in the laboratory. _____

2 You **should** leave your dog outside. _____

3 You **shouldn't** wear outdoor shoes on the squash courts. _____

4 You **can** park your car here for up to half an hour. _____

5 You **must** show your ID when entering and leaving the building. _____

6 You **must not** skateboard inside the building. _____

9.2 PROHIBITION, PERMISSION, OBLIGATION (PAST) (PAGE 89)

Prohibition, permission, obligation (past)	
We can use a range of expressions to talk about permission, prohibition, and obligation in the past.	
Permission	*could, were allowed to*
Prohibition	*couldn't, were not allowed to*
Obligation	*had to, were required to, were supposed to* note: *were required to* is stronger than *were supposed to*

A **Complete the sentences using an appropriate expression from the grammar chart.**

1 When we were kids, we _____ stay up after 10 o'clock. If we did, we got in trouble.

2 At school, we _____ wear a uniform at all times. They were very strict about it.

3 When I was in high school, I _____ play video games on school nights before I did my homework.

4 When I was a teenager, I _____ come home by nine o'clock on weekends, but sometimes I stayed out later.

10.1 PAST UNREAL CONDITIONALS (PAGE 99)

Past unreal conditionals	
Past unreal conditionals refer to imagined past situations. They have two parts:	
The *if* clause introduces or describes an **imagined situation.**	The main clause asks about or discusses **an imagined result.**
The verb is in the past perfect, but it refers to a hypothetical time, NOT a past time.	Use the modal verb *would* + *have* + past participle for statements, questions, and short answers.

Statement	If I **had studied** more in college,	I **would have gotten** better grades.
	If they **hadn't dug** a well,	they **wouldn't have found** the terracotta army.
Question	If you **had studied** more,	**would** you **have gotten** better grades?
Short answers	Yes, I **would / might have.**	No, I **wouldn't / might not have.**

When the *if* clause comes first, it ends with a comma:

    If you had gone with us, you would have seen it for yourself.

When the main clause comes first, no comma is necessary:

    You would have seen it for yourself if you had gone with us.

Use *might* instead of *would* when you're not sure about the result:

    You might have learned something if you had gone with us.

A   **Complete the sentences using the correct form of the verbs in parentheses ( ).**

1 If he _____ (not have) an accident on the way to the meeting,
  he _____ (not arrive) late.

2 If she _____ (stay) in school and _____ (get) her
  degree, they _____ (hire) her.

3 If they _____ (not discover) the cause of the infection, many more people
  _____ (die).

4 If I _____ (not go) on vacation to Florida, I _____
  (never meet) my wife!

10.2 MODALS OF PAST PROBABILITY (PAGE 101)

Modals of past probability
We use *should have* to evaluate or criticize past actions.
I **should have bought** that apartment. = It was a mistake not to buy that apartment.
I **shouldn't have made** that mistake.
We use *could / might have* to talk about something that was possible but didn't happen. You can use *couldn't have* to talk about something that wasn't possible.
I **could have worked** harder, but I didn't bother.
I **couldn't have caught** that plane. I woke up too late.
We often contract *have* when using past modals in speech but not in writing.
"You **should've told** me you were busy."
"I **shouldn't've gone** out last night."

A **Rewrite the sentences using past modals.**

I chose not to study medicine in college. → *I could have studied medicine in college.*

1 It wasn't a good idea to go out the night before the exam. → I shouldn't …
2 I'm sorry that I didn't call you last night. → I …
3 I didn't check the weather forecast and I brought all the wrong clothes. → I …
4 There was a chance of getting that job if I'd really tried. → I …
5 It's not possible for him to come to the U.S. because he doesn't have a visa. → He …

11.1 GERUND AND INFINITIVE AFTER *FORGET, REMEMBER, STOP* (PAGE 109)

A **Choose the correct form of the verb to complete the sentences.**

1 Everyone stopped *talking / to talk* and turned to look at the man who had just walked in.
2 I was feeling hungry, so I stopped *getting / to get* something to eat.
3 I remember *seeing / to see* him for the first time. It was like meeting my twin!
4 I remembered *buying / to buy* a birthday present for my brother this year! He's going to be so happy!
5 Did you forget *locking / to lock* the door? Look, it's wide open!
6 I'll never forget *playing / to play* in the snow at my uncle's farmhouse.

11.2 CAUSATIVE VERBS: *HELP, LET, MAKE* (page 111)

A **Complete the sentences with *help, let, make* and the correct personal pronoun.**

1 My dad's great with engines. He can _____ fix your car.
2 My parents were pretty strict. They never _____ stay out late with my friends.
3 He's so good with computers. He _____ build my own website in, like, an hour!
4 They really love that dog. They even _____ ride in the front seat of the car.
5 My big brother used to be a real bully. He used to _____ do all his homework for him!
6 We're moving into a new apartment this weekend. Could you _____ carry some boxes and stuff?

12.1 ADDING EMPHASIS (PAGE 119)

Adding emphasis

To add emphasis, you can start a statement with a phrase that alerts the listener to the special information about to come. The emphasis phrase usually takes one of two forms:

What I + verb (+ *about*)   **OR**   *The thing I* + verb (+ *about*)

The verb *be* (in the appropriate form) connects the emphasis phrase with the thing you want to emphasize or point you want to make.

emphasis phrase	*be*	point/thing you want to emphasize
What I love about Spanish food	is	all the different kinds of tapas.
The thing I enjoy about running	is	getting outside in the fresh air.
What I didn't know	was	the door was locked!
The thing I liked most about living in California	was	the weather.

A   **Rewrite sentences using the expression in parentheses ( ). Make any changes needed to the sentences.**

1   I really liked the smell in that shop. (*What I …*)
2   The food was the best thing about the trip. (*The thing I …*)
3   I remember there was a beautiful beach in that area. (*What I …*)
4   It was a good band, but we especially liked the singer's voice. (*The thing we …*)
5   I really miss my grandma's cooking. (*What I …*)
6   From childhood I remember my first bicycle. (*The thing I …*)

12.2 SUBSTITUTION AND REFERENCING (PAGE 121)

A   **Read the paragraph and <u>underline</u> unnecessary repetition. Then rewrite the paragraph using referencing and substitution to avoid the repetition.**

Your podcast on false memories was very interesting. But it really made me question the reliability of my own memories. If my own memories aren't reliable, then how can I learn from my past? I've tried to learn lessons from my mistakes. But what if I can't remember my mistakes correctly? If I can't remember my mistakes correctly, are the lessons that I learn really lessons? Maybe some lessons are based on accurate memories and other lessons are based on false memories. How could I tell the accurate lesson from the false lessons? Just thinking about whether my memories are accurate or whether my memories are inaccurate has gotten me really confused.

VOCABULARY PRACTICE

7.1 DESCRIBING COMMUNICATION (PAGE 66)

A **Choose the correct preposition in each sentence.**

1 He never replied *with / to* my email.

2 I was informed *by / of* the problem too late.

3 We had a nice time at the family reunion. It was great to catch up *in / with* all my cousins.

B **Complete the opinions with a reporting verb from the box in the correct form. What other reporting verbs might be possible in each context?**

catch up with	comment	congratulate	contact	criticize
explain	gossip	inform of	keep in touch with	mention
persuade	reply to	report	respond to	

1 "A good thing about social media is that you can read a post and then _____ on it. Other people might then _____ your comments. You get to know a lot of people that way!"

2 "I use social media to _____ people on their birthdays and to _____ _____ my friends, to find out what's happening with them."

3 "I never _____ about people's private lives or _____ people on social media. That's not nice, and it also isn't fair."

4 "It's hard to _____ somebody to use social media if they don't like the idea. You can _____ why you like it, but they probably won't care!"

7.2 COMMUNICATING ONLINE (PAGE 68)

A **Match words from the box with their definitions.**

clickbait	geo-tag	hashtag	lifecaster	lurker
meme	newsfeed	podcaster	profile	status update
tag	timeline	trending topic		

1 part of a website that updates often to show the latest news _____

2 a person who produces audio stories to download or stream online _____

3 the newest information that you post online _____

4 someone who puts everything about themselves on social media _____

5 internet content that encourages people to click on particular links _____

6 a story or news item that has become popular on social media _____

7 biographical information that you post on social media _____

8 add someone's name to your post or photo on social media _____

B **Use the other words in the box to complete the post about online communication.**

Distractions! They're everywhere online. It could be a friend asking for donations to support them in a charity fun run, but then again, it could be a new [1] _____ that everyone is now using in their messages! It might be a really funny [2] _____ that has gone viral overnight. There could be a review that you posted online and now have to [3] _____ to show a location for it. In fact it could be anything – a text, an image, a video that you just have to put on your [4] _____ right now!

This is hard for all of us. Sometimes it's good to disconnect from social media for a while. Or, if that's too hard, just don't post for a while. Be a [5] _____ and enjoy a view of the digital world from a distance!

8.1 DESCRIBING JOBS (PAGE 76)

A **Find words in the box to match the definitions.**

challenging	desk job	dream job	freelance	full-time
government job	high-paying	main job	part-time	permanent
second job	stressful	temporary	tiring	tough

1 It only lasts a few months. _____
2 This means there are often a lot of problems to deal with. _____
3 You get a good salary. _____
4 You only work a few hours. _____
5 This is what you've always wanted to do. _____
6 This means you work in an office. _____
7 You usually have one of these to get some extra money. _____
8 You don't have a contract with one company, but instead you work for different companies. _____

B **Choose the best word to complete the description. Can you guess the job?**

The first few years in the job were really ¹*part-time / tough*. I had to work very long hours and it was physically ²*tiring / freelance*. It's the total opposite of a ³*desk job / temporary job*. But I loved it! It wasn't very ⁴*permanent / high-paying* to start with, but as I progressed through my career my salary grew very quickly. When I got married and had kids I decided to reduce my hours and work ⁵*a second job / part-time*. I'm so grateful to the hospital for letting me do that.

8.2 TALKING ABOUT WORK/LIFE BALANCE (PAGE 78)

A **Complete the sentences with the words and phrases in the box.**

9-to-5	always connected	assignments	busy schedule
family life	seminar	office hours	social life

1 I have such a _____ at the moment. I don't have time for anything but work!
2 I've been traveling a lot for work recently, and it's really affecting my _____ . I hardly ever see my kids these days!
3 Don't call too early. Our _____ are 10 a.m. to 6 p.m.
4 My new job is great, and it's having a really positive effect on my _____ . I go out with my coworkers all the time!
5 I can't believe it. Our professor just gave us three _____ to do over the weekend!
6 I really envy you with your _____ job. I have to work nights and weekends.
7 I love teaching online, but it means I'm _____ . It's really difficult for me to get away from my computer.
8 This is going to be a tough semester. I have five regular classes, but I'm also taking a _____ on business ethics Tuesday nights.

B **Match the words and phrases with their definitions.**

> downtime   time off   commitments   seminar   chill out   shift

1 things that you have agreed or arranged to do _____
2 the period of time a person is scheduled to work _____
3 a time when you can relax _____
4 a meeting of a group of people with a teacher _____
5 a period of time when you do not work due to illness or vacations _____
6 rest, relax, or be calm _____

9.1 TALKING ABOUT PLACES (PAGE 86)

A **Match the places in the box with their descriptions.**

> arts center   boardwalk   city hall   construction site   consulate
> courthouse   highway rest stop   laboratory   playground   public space
> residential area   toll plaza

1 a park or square or other outdoor place _____
2 a place where children love to go _____
3 where scientists do experiments _____
4 where people live _____
5 where you stop to pay so that you can use the highway _____
6 where you can take painting classes or see a play _____

B **Read the quotes. Use the other places in the box to say where each person is.**
1 "We've been driving a long time and need a break." _____
2 "I'm sorry, but you have to wear a hard hat. It can be dangerous." _____
3 "I've come to get a visa for my trip to Egypt." _____
4 "We'll go swimming later. Let's get some ice cream and walk for a while." _____
5 "Could you tell me if this is the right place to apply for a parking permit?" _____
6 "My mom works here. She's a judge." _____

9.2 TALKING ABOUT RULES (PAGE 89)

A **Choose the correct word to complete the sentences.**
1 Speed limit signs are used to *control / prohibit* traffic within the downtown area.
2 You cannot park your car here unless you have *obligation / permission* from the central office.
3 All guests are required to *limit / register* at reception on arrival.
4 There is a *ban / requirement* on all ball sports in all residential areas.

B **Complete the sentences with the correct form of the word in parentheses ( ).**
1 Swimming in the lake is strictly _____ (prohibit) at all times.
2 You must consider all the legal _____ (require) when starting a business.
3 Click here to start your _____ (register) process.
4 The bus is _____ (limit) to 50 passengers!

10.1 TALKING ABOUT DISCOVERIES (PAGE 98)

A **Complete the sentences with the nouns in the box.**

> breakthrough   challenge   connection   discovery   insight
> knowledge   phenomenon   research   solution

1 They have made a great _____ in AIDS research, but there is still no cure.
2 It's a very difficult task, but now I'm ready to take on the _____ .
3 Politicians have discussed it, but they have not provided a _____ to the problem yet.
4 The documentary was fascinating. It provides real _____ into this complex issue.
5 If you get the scholarship, you'll have to carry out your own _____ .
6 The crime rate is rising, and experts are investigating this _____ at the moment.
7 Detectives have noticed the _____ between the crime rate and high unemployment.
8 The internet provided me with the _____ that I needed to complete our report.
9 Like so many others in the past, they made the _____ accidentally.

B **Choose the correct words to complete the sentences.**

1 We *faced / noticed* a terrible challenge, but we achieved our goal in the end.
2 People are *making / finding* new discoveries in the natural sciences all the time.
3 If you *provide / gain* us with the knowledge we need, we'll accomplish the task.
4 Scientists are still *noticing / making* breakthroughs in the world of medicine.
5 Investigators *noticed / faced* this phenomenon, but they didn't know how best to react to it.
6 The program helped me *gain / carry out* vital insights into this problem.
7 A lot of researchers don't realize they've *made / investigated* a breakthrough until much later.
8 They *carried out / provided* the academic research, but they haven't studied the results yet.
9 We'll need to *find / make* a solution soon, or this problem could get out of hand.

10.2 DISCUSSING RIGHT AND WRONG (PAGE 100)

A **Choose the correct words to complete the sentences.**

1 "I'm sorry, it was a complete *confusion / misunderstanding* on my part. I hadn't read the report properly."
2 "I deserve all the *mistake / blame*. I'm the one who broke the vase."
3 "I managed to correct that *fault / error* and now I feel much better."
4 "Rob was reading the wrong page of the instructions, which caused a lot of *blunder / confusion*."
5 "If you can *fail / fix* that little mistake, you'll pass the exam easily."

B **Use the words in the box to replace the underlined words in each sentence.**

> ~~blunder~~   an epic fail   fault   make this right   mixed up

  blunder
1 "I can't believe they made such a stupid ~~mistake~~."

2 "I feel terrible. I have to find a way to <u>correct the situation</u>."

3 "Sorry I missed our meeting. I got the dates <u>switched</u>."

4 "My attempt to cook a fancy dinner for my girlfriend was <u>a complete disaster</u>."

5 "I didn't complete the report on time. It's my <u>responsibility</u>."

11.1 TALKING ABOUT COLLEGE EDUCATION (PAGE 108)

A **Match the words in the box with their definitions. There is one extra.**

> dorm   faculty   freshman   grade
> major   semester   society

1 the teachers in a college department
2 a first-year college student
3 a club that is organized by students
4 a building where many students live
5 the main focus of your studies in college
6 a letter or number that shows how good your work is

B **Complete the sentences with the words in the box.**

> associations   campus   degree
> facilities   professors   undergraduate

1 We have some amazing sports _____ on _____ .
2 Our _____ are awesome! They're so helpful and supportive.
3 I'm an _____ . After I get my _____ in biology, I'm going to go to medical school.
4 There are so many different student _____ . It's really difficult to choose just one!

11.2 TALKING ABOUT SCIENCE (PAGE 110)

A **Match words from the chart to their definitions.**

abstract noun	verb	person	adjective	compound adjective
science		scientist	scientific	scientifically-proven
research	research	researcher		research-based
proof	prove		proven	scientifically-proven
base/basis	base		based (on facts)	science-based
medicine			medical	medically-approved

1 a person who works in a laboratory conducting experiments
2 the set of facts that show something is true
3 the study of the human body and how to repair it
4 the study of natural things
5 a person who studies natural things
6 when doctors say that something is good for their patients

B **Complete the sentences with the correct form of the word in parentheses ( ).**

1 The researchers were not able to _____ (proof) that cheese gives you nightmares.
2 It is a _____ (science) fact that carrots can improve your night vision.
3 _____ (medicine) studies suggest that mosquitoes prefer certain blood types.
4 The fact that honey calms a cough has been _____ (science) proven.
5 Studies _____ (base) on a small number of patients are never totally reliable.

12.1 TALKING ABOUT THE SENSES (PAGE 118)

A   **Match the adjectives to the nouns. More than one answer may be possible.**

1 stinky _____
2 colorful _____
3 damp _____
4 musty _____
5 melodic _____
6 bright _____
7 tasty _____
8 high-pitched _____
9 deep _____
10 flavorful _____

a trash
b towel
c voices
d clothes
e cookies

B   **Choose the correct words to complete the sentences.**

1 I play the bass guitar because I like its rich, *deep / damp* sound.
2 I woke up to the *melodic / high-pitched* scream of the fire alarm.
3 After shaving, my skin feels so *smooth / rough*.
4 The boxes from the basement are so *deep / musty*. Open a window!
5 The omelets at that restaurant are more *bright / flavorful* than you can believe!

12.2 DESCRIBING MEMORIES (PAGE 120)

A   **Complete the sentences with the correct form of a word or phrase from the box. More than one answer may be possible.**

bring back	childhood	clear	distant
early	long-term	look back on	recall
recent	recognize	remind	short-term
vague	vivid		

1 We met at Sam's party? Really? I was so tired that night. I only have a _____ memory of the party, but no memory at all of the people there.
2 I don't like to _____ unhappy times from my _____. Best just to move on and forget about it.
3 After all these years, I didn't _____ her face, but I remembered her voice!
4 I have a really _____ memory of the first time we met. I can even remember exactly what you were wearing.
5 That song always _____ me of the summer of 2005.

B   **Choose the correct words to complete the sentences.**

1 It was 20 years ago that I lived there, so it's just a *distant / early* memory now.
2 My grandma is losing her *short-term / long-term* memory, but she remembers her childhood very well, so her *short-term / long-term* memory is still great.
3 What's the first thing you can *bring back / recall* about your early years?
4 I have a very *early / vague* memory, but it might be false. I was four, and I was at the zoo with my mother. We were looking at the lions and eating popcorn. I can see it so clearly in my mind. The strange thing is, she doesn't *recognize / recall* this at all.
5 Of all the senses, smell *brings back / looks back on* the most *vague / vivid* memories.

PROGRESS CHECK

Can you do these things? Check (✓) what you can do. Then write your answers in your notebook.

Now I can ...	Prove it
☐ use verbs and verb phrases to describe communication.	Write at least five sentences about how and why you communicate with people who are far away.
☐ report statements that were made in different tenses.	Listen to a conversation and make notes. Report what each person said using reporting verbs.
☐ use terms for different types of online communication.	Write six sentences about different aspects of your own online communication habits.
☐ report questions that were asked in different tenses.	Complete the reported question: "Do you prefer one big test or six small ones?" *Their teacher asked _____ one big test or six small ones.*
☐ recount conversations, news, and stories.	Recount something you experienced in story form using appropriate expressions to indicate different speakers.
☐ write an email in both a formal and informal register.	Look at your emails from lesson 7.4. Can you make them better? Find three ways.

Now I can ...	Prove it
☐ use terms to describe jobs and work situations.	Describe the jobs or work situations of three people you know using the terms from the lesson.
☐ use present unreal conditionals.	Write three questions about what someone might or might not do today.
☐ discuss work/life balance.	Write six sentences about your work/life balance.
☐ express dissatisfaction with *I wish*.	Complete the wishes: I waste so much time playing video games. → *I wish I _____ so much time playing video games.* It's so cold outside. → *I wish it _____ warmer outside.*
☐ talk through options to reach a decision.	Present and discuss three possible ways to address a situation, and encourage or discourage each of them.
☐ write a response to comments on a podcast.	Look at your response from lesson 8.4. Can you make it better? Find three ways.

Now I can ...	Prove it
☐ use nouns and compound nouns to name different places.	List five places that have rules and regulations about behavior.
☐ express present prohibition, permission, and obligation.	Write one rule for each place on your list (see previous line) using different structures.
☐ use different word forms to discuss rules.	Write one sentence for each word (in any form): limit, ban, control, permit, require.
☐ express prohibition, permission, and obligation in the past.	Write six sentences about rules and freedoms in your childhood using different structures.
☐ use phrases to make generalizations.	Generalize about your culture or region. Contrast the information with another culture if you can.
☐ write a message registering a complaint.	Look at your message from lesson 9.4. Can you make it better? Find three ways.

PROGRESS CHECK

Can you do these things? Check (✓) what you can do. Then write your answers in your notebook.

Now I can ...

☐ use verb + noun phrases to describe investigation and discovery.

☐ use past unreal conditionals to discuss present outcomes.

☐ use words for different kinds of mistakes and for corrections.

☐ use modals of past probability to suggest unreal alternatives.

☐ keep a listener engaged by using phrases to hold their attention.

☐ write a comment about things you can and can't live without.

Prove it

Describe the discovery of microwaves or the terracotta army in your own words but using phrases from the lesson.

Write three sentences about how something in your life today would be different if past events had happened differently.

Use a variety of words to tell the story of a big mistake you or someone you know made and how it turned out in the end.

Think of three alternative historical outcomes. For example: *If the U.S hadn't bought Alaska in 1867, it might have joined Canada.*

Tell a story and use phrases to keep your listener engaged. Show interest in someone else's story.

Look at your comment from lesson 10.4. Can you make it better? Find three ways.

Now I can ...

☐ use terms to describe the college experience.

☐ change the meaning of *forget*, *remember*, and *stop*.

☐ use different word forms to discuss science and medicine.

☐ use *help, let*, and *make* to indicate cause and effects.

☐ discuss alternatives and give recommendations.

☐ write a comment presenting an argument.

Prove it

Use your imagination to describe a day in the life of a college student using at least eight vocabulary words.

Write two logical sentences with *forget, remember*, and *stop* followed by a gerund in one sentence and an infinitive in the other.

Write five sentences using five different vocabulary words, one each for abstract noun, verb, person, adjective, and compound adjective.

Use *help, let*, and *make* once each to give advice. For example: *If you show your ID card, the guard lets you cut through the building.*

Suggest three alternative routes and present the advantages and disadvantages of each. End with a personal recommendation.

Look at your comment from lesson 11.4. Can you make it better? Find three ways.

Now I can ...

☐ use sense adjectives for descriptions.

☐ emphasize something using the structure *What I remember most is ...* or *The thing I liked was ...*

☐ use words to describe and share memories.

☐ use substitution and referencing to avoid repetition.

☐ prompt and recall shared memories.

☐ write a summary and response paragraph.

Prove it

Write six sentences using sense adjectives to describe someone else's home, now or in the past.

Write three sentences emphasizing particular things about the home you described (see previous line).

Write five sentences about an event that you remember differently from someone else. Write from your perspective only.

Use substitution and referencing to explain how the other person remembers the event differently (see previous line).

Write three ways to prompt someone else's memory about a shared experience. Write two ways to share a similar experience.

Look at your summary and response paragraph from lesson 12.4. Can you make it better? Find three ways.

PAIR WORK PRACTICE (STUDENT A)

7.3 EXERCISE 4A (PAGE 71)   STUDENT A

Story 1: A person won a prize unexpectedly

Gabrielle (a girl you both know) won the first prize at a school art contest out of twenty candidates. She only started painting a year ago but has a natural talent. You heard she painted a portrait of her father.

Story 2: A birthday party that ended in disaster

Marcus' birthday party ended in disaster. He was blowing out the candles on his birthday cake, and one fell on the floor and set some newspapers on fire. You don't know if anyone was hurt. None of Marcus' presents was damaged, not even his new toy fire truck.

Story 3: Road trouble

Someone told you that the Carter family was driving across the U.S. for their summer vacation. In the middle of the Arizona desert, they got a flat tire. They tried to change the tire, but the spare tire was also flat. Finally, another car came along and took them to a town to get help. You don't know if they are home or still on vacation.

PAIR WORK PRACTICE (STUDENT B)

7.3   EXERCISE 4A (PAGE 71)   STUDENT B

Story 1: A person won a prize unexpectedly

Gabrielle (a girl you both know) won first prize at a school painting contest. At just 13, she was the youngest person in the competition. This was the first time she had entered the competition. You heard she painted a landscape of the area near her house.

Story 2: A birthday party that ended in disaster

Marcus' birthday party ended in disaster. There was a fire at the house, but you don't know what started the fire. They had to evacuate the house, but nobody was hurt.

Story 3: Road trouble

Jane Carter told you last month that they were going to drive somewhere for their summer vacation, but you don't remember where. You saw Jane Carter at the supermarket just yesterday, and she told you that they had had some car problems, but they were all fine and very happy to be home.